TRASH CAN TOYS AND GAMES

TRASH CAN TOYS AND GAMES

by Leonard Todd

Drawings by
chas. b. slackman

Photographs by
Carl Fischer

A
Subsistence Press
Book

The Viking Press
New York

Copyright © 1974 by Subsistence Press.
All rights reserved.
First published in 1974 by The Viking Press, Inc.
625 Madison Avenue, New York, N.Y. 10022.
Published simultaneously in Canada by
The Macmillan Company of Canada Limited.
SBN 670-72433-5
Library of Congress catalog card number: 73-3953
Printed in U.S.A.

Design: Samuel N. Antupit

Special Thanks

to Herbie, who tried to help but got arrested for "stealing" trash from a neighbor's garbage; to Tom, who contributed his expertise and a roller skate; to toymakers Dan, Sarina, and Lin; to friends at Service Dairies and Perrone's Fruit Market; to Sandy, who offered the contents of her trash can; to Lena-Miles and Leonard, who offered their ideas; to Charles, for his drawings; to Carl, for his photographs; to Sam, the designer; to Jamie, the editor;

and to Catharine.

Contents

PREFACE

Let's face it: trash is here to stay. The more advanced our society becomes, the more trash we make. New methods of disposing of it will be discovered, perhaps, but no matter how many gains are made, there will always be an enormous amount of trash with which to contend —trash that can litter our streets, spot our countryside, pollute our streams.

Trash doesn't have to be harmful, however. It can be useful if it is reclaimed and turned into new products. First, of course, it has to be picked up. After all, a metal can can't be recycled while it is lying along the roadside; a bottle can't be reused if it is left at a picnic site; old paper can't be reclaimed when it is clogging the gutters. Picking up all this litter is going to be a heavy job, so we might as well look for ways to enjoy it.

The best way to make fun of trash is to turn it into toys and games. And that's what this book is all about. It is divided into seven parts, each of which deals with a different kind of litter and the toys that can be made from it. The seven litter materials are wood, paper, paperboard, cloth, glass, plastics, and metals. Some of the toys that can be constructed from these materials are traditional ones, like the wooden skatemobile; others, like the plastic space station, have been newly designed for this book by the author.

You won't need any special tools to build the toys—just a pair of scissors, a knife, a hammer, a saw, some sandpaper, and several types of glue. You will, however, need lots of trash, everything from metal cans and wooden crates to plastic caps and paperboard boxes. But don't worry about the supply. Until everyone else learns how much fun litter can be, you'll be able to find all you need almost without trying. As you collect, you may find trash items that are not mentioned in this book. No problem. Save them anyway and invent your own toys.

When you find something you can use, bring it home and clean it thoroughly. Set up boxes to hold your finds, one for each of the seven litter materials, a kind of trash file. Sorting the trash in this way is one more step in getting it ready to be recycled, since the limitations of present-day technology make it necessary to separate the various kinds of litter before they can be reclaimed. Glass has to be separated from metals, and metals have to be separated from plastics, and so on. When you're finished with your toys, take them apart and deliver each trash file to the appropriate recycling center.

Of course, you won't be able to solve the problem of solid waste disposal simply by making toys. But you'll help. And you'll have fun trying.

WOOD

When the pioneers first came to America, they used wood from the forests to make log cabins, rail fences, wagons, tables, benches, and beds. And they burned wood to cook food and keep warm. The forests seemed vast enough to last forever, but bit by bit, tree by tree, great stretches of fine timberland were destroyed.

We know now that the forests don't last forever. We know that if we continue to cut so many trees so carelessly, our woodlands will disappear completely. So we have begun to plant new trees to replace the ones we cut down.

Like the early settlers we depend on wood a great deal, especially for building homes and making paper. But in certain cases we have found that other materials will serve us just as well. For example, many containers and small household items that were once made of wood are now made from less expensive plastics and paperboard.

This substitution of materials has had a sad effect on toys that were traditionally made from wooden throwaways. Some of the toys, in fact, have entirely disappeared as their wooden sources have been phased out. Happily, one source of wood for toys, the fruit crate, is still around. For generations crates have been used to make scooters, doll cradles, dog houses, shoe-shine stands. Crates, too, are being replaced by paperboard boxes, but since certain fruits need the air circulation that openwork wood containers provide, crates will be with us for a while longer.

The trash pile outside the grocery store is the place to find these crates, as well as wooden fruit baskets and berry boxes. All wooden containers make good toys, so ask your grocer to save them for you.

Tony's Sensational Skatemobile

In the early 1930s a young boy named Tony lived in Chicago. His family was poor, and Tony had few toys. He did have one roller skate, but everyone told him that it was worthless, that it was like having one chopstick, that he might as well throw it away. Tony was stubborn, however, and he kept his roller skate.

There were plenty of wooden crates around the city in those days, and Tony often played with them. Soon he got the idea of combining a crate, a 2 x 4 board, and his roller skate to make a sort of scooter. It worked. It was the world's first skatemobile.

Tony's invention caused a sensation. Within a week there were skatemobiles all over Chicago; and within a few years they were being enjoyed all across the country. And it all started with a "worthless" roller skate!

To build a skatemobile of your own, you will need a 3-foot length of 2 x 4 wooden board, a 24-inch length of broom handle, some

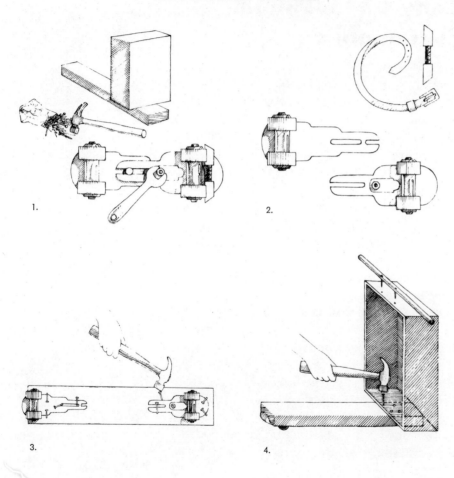

1.

2.

3.

4.

nails, and a strong wooden crate, about 24 inches long, 12 inches wide, and 10 inches deep. Most important, you, like Tony, will need a single roller skate.

The first step is to take the skate apart by loosening the adjustment screw that holds the front and rear portions together (see figure 1). Separate the two pieces and place one at one end of the 2 x 4 and one at the other, as shown in the drawing. Attach the rear skate wheels first. The heel plate of the roller skate should overlap the back end of the 2 x 4. Hammer several nails into the board around the skate plate and in its open slot. Then bend the nails down over the metal plate to hold it in place (figure 3). If you wish to make it even more secure, wrap the skate strap around the board and the skate plate and buckle it tightly, cutting off any extra strap that might drag on the ground. Next attach the front skate wheels. Place them on the front end of the board, hammer in the nails, and bend the nails over to secure the plate as before.

Now nail the crate onto the front of the board (figure 4) to form the hood. If you like, you can nail a small crate—an asparagus box is perfect—onto the back to make a seat. Then nail the broomstick handlebars onto the hood and bend the nails under against the inside of the crate. That's all there is to it. You're ready to ride. But stay off busy streets, because these old-fashioned vehicles are not designed to compete with automobiles. They're safest on sidewalks without pedestrians or in empty driveways.

Finally, you can jazz up your skatemobile with paint and reflectors and lanterns and flags and license plates and streamers and horns.

Crate Construction

Wooden crates are just right for constructing model buildings of all kinds. You can make sprawling factories, farms, and schools. But you'd be wise to start with something simple, such as a house, because building with crates is hard work and takes a lot of time.

Ask your grocer for at least four or five large crates—the kind melons come in are best—and a few shallow crates, such as the ones grapes are shipped in. One or two of the melon crates you will take apart and use for roofing, porches, fences, etc.

To take a crate apart, follow this special method: First gently hammer the inside of the box, where the surfaces are nailed together, in order to separate slightly the pieces of wood from one another. Then hammer the wood, but not the nails, back together. Finally, pull out the nailheads with the claw end of a hammer. Leave a couple of corners intact to use for gables or roof supports.

To build a house, stack and arrange several large crates, open sides toward you, to make what architects call a cross-section. A cross-section is a view of a building with the outside wall removed in order to let you see inside. In arranging the cross-section, remember that you can divide a crate in half to make two rooms if the crate is used horizontally, or an upstairs and a downstairs, if the crate is used vertically (see figure 1). Once you have settled on an arrangement, set the crates up on a base made from the grape crates and nail all the parts together.

Now line the insides of the crates with stiff corrugated paperboard. Cut each piece so that it will fit snugly into the crates. To make a dividing wall or floor, cut two pieces of paperboard the same width and depth as the crate. Glue strips of paperboard about ½ inch wide in a zigzag pattern on one piece of board (see figure 2), then glue the other piece on top of the strips. The strips will separate the two pieces of board, giving the divider thickness and making it rigid. Slide this new floor or wall into the crate and glue it in place. Fill in the open end of the divider with a strip of paperboard.

There are several ways to make a roof for the house. One easy method is to take the corner pieces from an extra crate and use

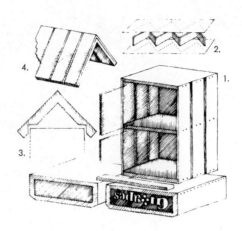

them as roof supports. Notch the supports where they meet the top corners of the crates, and nail or glue them in place as shown in figure 3, one at each end of the roof area. The open gable ends can be filled in with corrugated paperboard. When the two supports are in place, cut two pieces of paperboard to form the front and rear roof surfaces. Glue or tack these onto the end supports, then glue slats from an extra crate, cut to size, to the paperboard to form the roof (see figure 4).

Throwaways will provide the furnishings for your model. Wrapping paper left over from birthdays and holidays can be wallpaper. Pieces of thick cloth or the patchworks on page 60 can be rugs. Use belt buckles to frame small pictures for the walls. Pipe cleaners threaded with beads can be curved into chandeliers. Matchboxes can be stacked up to form stairs. Even plastic bottle caps can be used, for dishes and pots in the kitchen. You'll find more ideas for furniture on page 90.

Basketbag

Outside every grocery store there is a pile of wooden baskets, the kind that fruit and vegetables come in. You can use these containers to play a game of skill called basketbag. The object of the game is to toss a bean bag into the containers, so you'll need about a dozen baskets of all sizes and shapes. You'll also need a large piece of plywood or an old door for a backboard.

Lay the plywood flat on the ground and put the baskets on top of it, open sides up. Arrange them close together, so that there is very little space in between. Some will have higher sides than others; but this will make no difference.

When the baskets are arranged in a pattern that pleases you, nail them onto the plywood. Now take a marking pen or a crayon and draw a big number in the bottom of each one. Use only numbers from 1 to 10, putting the higher numbers in the smaller baskets and the lower numbers in the bigger baskets.

To make a beanbag, take an old sock and fill it about half full with seeds and beans that you have gathered yourself. If it's not a

BASKETBAG.

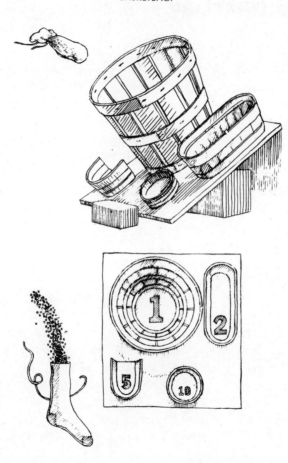

good season for beans, you can buy inexpensive packages of them at the grocery store. Cut off the unused part of the sock and sew up the beans with a needle and thread. Or you can use string to tie the open of the sock together.

Lean the game board against a wall at a slight slant and put some bricks in front of it to hold it in place. Draw a line on the ground about ten giant steps back from the board. Now you're ready to test your skill.

Any number up to five or six can play. Each should have a beanbag of a different color. To begin, all players stand together along the line and on a signal try to toss their beanbags at the same time into the baskets. The better your aim, the smaller the basket you can shoot for, and, if successful, the higher you will score. Each person gets the number of points marked on the basket in which his bag lands. If a player does not bag a basket at all, he loses one point. Anything goes. But you only get points if your bag makes a basket; and you always lose a point if it doesn't. The first player to reach 100 is the winner.

Basketball

A hundred years ago, there was no ball game that could be played indoors. People tried to play football and soccer inside during the winter months, but too many windows were broken and too many bodies bruised on the hard wooden floors. Then, in 1891, James Naismith, a physical-education instructor at the YMCA training school in Springfield, Massachusetts, invented an indoor ball game that called for tossing a large ball through a goal. Naismith asked the superintendent of the gymnasium for two boxes to use for goals. The superintendent had no boxes, but he did have two half-bushel peach baskets, which he thought might work just as well. They did, and the game became known as basketball.

Today metal rims with nets are used instead of peach baskets. They are sometimes expensive, though, and there is no reason why you can't play basketball the original way, using a wooden basket from which the bottom has been removed. Nail the basket securely to a plywood backboard, then nail the backboard up onto a tree or the garage, and you're ready to play.

Though the peach basket will eventually wear out, a faulty basket is a whole lot better than none at all; and when it does wear out, just nail up another one.

Spool Racer

The spool racer is a traditional homemade toy, one that's been enjoyed by generations of toymakers. To build it, you'll need a large wooden spool, two pushpins, a medium-sized button, a strong rubber band, and an ice-cream stick.

First prepare the ice-cream stick (or any piece of light wood about 4½ inches long) by cutting a small notch on each side of it about 1 inch from one end. Prepare the button by carving a large single hole in its center with a knife. For most buttons this means simply joining together the holes that are already there. Now take the two pushpins and stick them into one end of the spool, on opposite sides of the hole, as shown in the drawing. Push them in only about three-quarters of the way. Wrap the rubber band around the pins and then thread it through the spool, through the button, and finally loop it around the notches in the stick. Wind up the stick, put the racer on a smooth surface, and Zoom!—there it goes.

Spool racers are so simple to build that you can soon have a whole fleet. To make

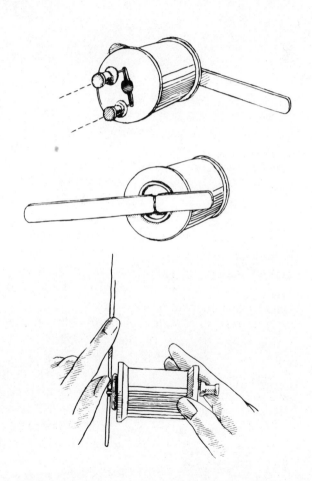

them easy to tell apart in a race, use different colors for pushpins and buttons. And try using a bead instead of a button for one of them. And try carving notches all around the rim of one spool to improve its climbing ability.

If you have trouble finding a wooden spool, you can use a plastic one, but you'll have to invent a replacement for the pushpins, since their points won't push into hard plastic. One solution is to slip a toothpick through a rubber band, then glue the pick over the center of the hole in the spool. This will hold the rubber band in place just as the pushpins did.

A spool racer sometimes has a way of heading off in directions that you never planned on, almost as if it were trying to do some exploring. Why not let it be a real explorer, then? Let it be a lunar rover and add it to the space station described on page 97. That way you can send it out from the station to gather important scientific information on its own. Or you can slide the station's astronaut onto the ice-cream stick after you've wound it up and let the rover carry him on secret missions far out in unknown territory.

Clothespin People

If you look carefully at an old-fashioned wooden clothespin, the kind without the metal spring, you'll see that it looks like a little person. It has a round head, a finely tapered body, and two long legs. All it needs is a pair of arms, which you can make easily from a pipe cleaner. You can buy packages of cleaners in different colors at any dime store.

To make the arms, take a pipe cleaner and at its mid-point loop it around the neck of the clothespin. Cross it tightly and twist it around a full turn. Bend up the ends to form hands, and then break off any excess.

To make the clothespin stand up by itself, cut out a piece of thin cardboard ¾ of an inch wide by 3 inches long. Score the cardboard with a knife at intervals of ¾ of an inch, so that it will fold, as shown in the diagram. Put two dots of glue on the cardboard and slip it between the feet of the clothespin to form a base.

Now give your clothespin a personality. First decide what you want it to be, then draw happy or sad or scowling features on the head with a ball-point pen. Finally, find a button or plastic cap that seems to suit the occasion and glue it on for a hat. There. A clothespin person is born.

Clothespin characters are great for acting out stories. And one of the best of the clothespin stories is "The Saga of the Blue Moon Saloon." It begins in a town in the Old West when Little Nell, the pretty schoolmarm, is kidnapped from the Blue Moon Saloon by grizzly old Snarl McGee. It's true that a nice girl like Nell shouldn't have been in the saloon in the first place, but, even so, she doesn't deserve to be carried off by Snarl McGee! Luckily, news of the dastardly deed reaches handsome Cowboy Sam, and he sets out to free the young lady. From then on it's a story of the battle between Good and Evil, Sam and Snarl. Little Nell, delighted by all the attention, is caught in the middle.

You can build the setting for this Western saga right in a cigar box. Just set the box on its side and open the front panel so that it is flat on the table, facing you. The box now forms an empty room which you can decorate and furnish and fill with people and action.

The photograph at the beginning of this chapter will give you the idea. It shows a cigar box fitted out as the Blue Moon Saloon, with all the furnishings constructed from throwaways. It can be made even fancier by adding two more cigar boxes, one on the right and one on the left, and letting their tops come together to form a peaked roof. Holes can be cut in these side walls to make windows and doors. To hold everything in place, glue the three boxes down onto a piece of corrugated cardboard.

Other cigar-box scenes from "The Saga of the Blue Moon Saloon" might take place in Little Nell's lacy living room or in Snarl's grubby mountain hideout. For outdoor scenes, you can build log cabins from ice-cream sticks, Indian tepees from conical paper cups, and fences from toothpicks or matchsticks.

The exciting climax of the saloon story will come when Snarl, in a final outburst of nastiness, ties the frantic Nell to the railroad tracks, with the Five O'Clock Special due any minute. It will be a close call for the clothespin schoolmarm, but Cowboy Sam will arrive in the nick of time. Then Little Nell will flutter her eyelashes; Sam will dust off his white hat; and poor old Snarl will mutter, "Curses! Foiled again!"

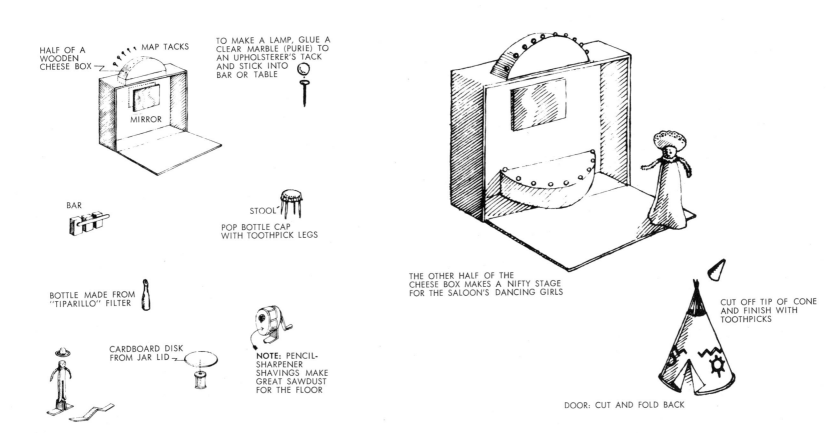

HALF OF A WOODEN CHEESE BOX

MAP TACKS

TO MAKE A LAMP, GLUE A CLEAR MARBLE (PURIE) TO AN UPHOLSTERER'S TACK AND STICK INTO BAR OR TABLE

MIRROR

BAR

STOOL

POP BOTTLE CAP WITH TOOTHPICK LEGS

BOTTLE MADE FROM "TIPARILLO" FILTER

CARDBOARD DISK FROM JAR LID

NOTE: PENCIL-SHARPENER SHAVINGS MAKE GREAT SAWDUST FOR THE FLOOR

THE OTHER HALF OF THE CHEESE BOX MAKES A NIFTY STAGE FOR THE SALOON'S DANCING GIRLS

CUT OFF TIP OF CONE AND FINISH WITH TOOTHPICKS

DOOR: CUT AND FOLD BACK

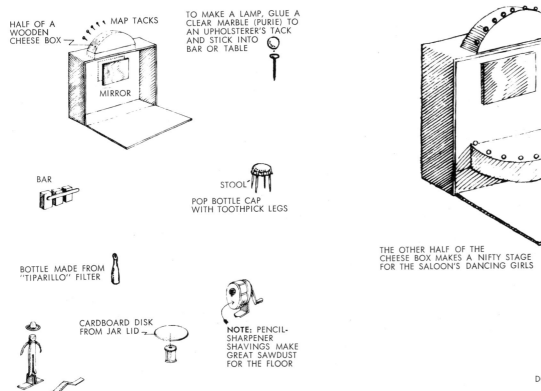

HALF OF A WOODEN CHEESE BOX

MAP TACKS

MIRROR

TO MAKE A LAMP, GLUE A CLEAR MARBLE (PURIE) TO AN UPHOLSTERER'S TACK AND STICK INTO BAR OR TABLE

BAR

STOOL

POP BOTTLE CAP WITH TOOTHPICK LEGS

BOTTLE MADE FROM "TIPARILLO" FILTER

CARDBOARD DISK FROM JAR LID

NOTE: PENCIL-SHARPENER SHAVINGS MAKE GREAT SAWDUST FOR THE FLOOR

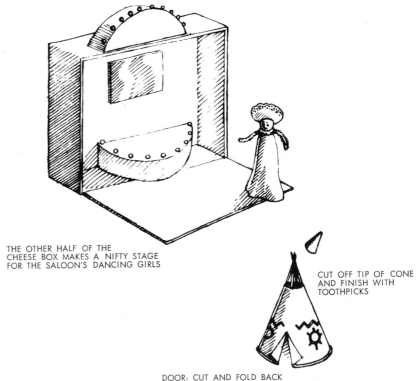

THE OTHER HALF OF THE CHEESE BOX MAKES A NIFTY STAGE FOR THE SALOON'S DANCING GIRLS

CUT OFF TIP OF CONE AND FINISH WITH TOOTHPICKS

DOOR: CUT AND FOLD BACK

PAPER

The first people to make paper weren't people at all. They were hornets. The female hornet is, in fact, a kind of paper machine. Using her jaws for a saw, she shaves tiny particles of wood off trees, then chews them up into pulp. As she builds her hive, she spreads the pulp out in thin layers, which dry into tough, springy coils of paper. It is said that in ancient times the Chinese learned the secret of papermaking by watching hornets at work.

The early Egyptians made paper, too; but they used a different process. They wove together thin strips of papyrus, a tall reed that grew in profusion along the banks of the Nile. The word papyrus is the source of our word for paper.

Today the papermaking process usually begins with logs cut in the forests. The wood is broken down into pulp, washed, bleached, and fed into a beater—a huge oval tub furnished with a kind of paddlewheel. The watery pulp is then refined, thinned, and pumped out onto a copper screen so finely woven that the pulp fibers remain on top while the water drains through. The pulp passes finally through a series of rollers, which squeeze out the extra wetness and little by little form it into paper.

Unfortunately the chemicals used in this process can pollute both water and air. It is only recently that paper mills have begun to install equipment to clean up the waste from the papermaking process before releasing it into our environment.

Since paper is easy to make, we use it for everything: for wrapping, for writing, for books, for labels, for decoration, even for money. Of course, this means that we throw away vast quantities of paper as well. In America alone about 60 billion pounds of paper and paperboard are discarded every year. This is equal to the weight of 8 million full-grown Indian elephants. What's more, since crumpled paper is bulky, it takes up a great deal more space than the elephants would.

Still, we don't have to be buried beneath all this waste paper. It can be put to better use. It can be collected and recycled into new paper. Recycling is carried out by first bleaching and shreading the old paper, then breaking it down chemically and adding it to virgin wood pulp at the beginning of the manufacturing process. And the paper that is produced can be very good. This book, in fact, is printed on paper that has been recycled.

Recycled paper makes sense from every point of view. But paper companies won't produce it unless they think the public wants it. You can help develop a market for it by using recycled stationery and notepaper. Your local conservation organization can tell you where to find it.

And you can start a miniature reclamation program of your own by using discarded paper to make the toys and games described in this chapter.

Paper-Bag Mask

DETAIL: EYELASH

The first paper bags were made in 1850. They were constructed entirely by hand, and so were relatively rare and expensive. It was not until 1876 that an automatic bag-making machine was invented, making it possible to mass produce paper bags.

Our great-grandparents valued paper bags and carefully saved them to use over and over again. We can follow this early example of recycling by finding second and even third uses for our bags. A grocery bag, for example, can be used again for a lunch sack and then again for a garbage bag. For fun, a paper bag can be used to make a mask.

To create a mask, choose a clean, sturdy bag that will fit over your head, and start designing a face for it. The eyes, mouth, and nose can be cut out with scissors and outlined with poster paints and crayons. Short fringes of paper can be added for eyelashes or mustaches; long fluttering paper strips can be pasted on for hair and beards.

There's really no limit to the different

masks you can design. You can do a curly-haired clown, a giraffe, an owl, and any number of monsters, even the ones from your own nightmares.

And when you're finished with a mask, you can stuff it with paper and staple it onto the end of a broom handle. Stuff an old shirt and a pair of trousers with paper and staple them onto the broomstick, too. Now you've got a scarecrow.

Hatful of News

What's a newspaper good for after it's been read? Making newspaper hats, for one thing. By working a few simple folds in the <u>Daily Gazette</u>, you can make a Dutch girl's bonnet, a Viking's helmet, Robin Hood's cap, even Napoleon's chapeau. You can be well dressed and well read at the same time.

To make a Napoleon's hat:
(1) Take a single sheet of newspaper, approximately 14 x 23 inches, and fold it as shown in figure 1.
(2) Fold the top corners down as in figure 2.
(3) Fold up the bottom edges of both the front and the back as in figure 3.

Glue the side flaps to each other, add a gold paper seal, and the hat is complete. Wear it as Napoleon himself would, with the points just above your ears, your hand inside your shirt front, and one foot on a big rock.

To make Robin Hood's cap, follow the same directions as above, but in step 3, fold the bottom pieces <u>twice</u> and tape their corners over each other as shown in the drawing. This

NAPOLEON'S HAT.

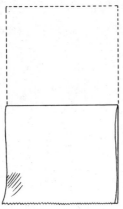

1.

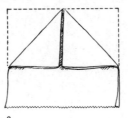

2.

3.

THIS HANDSOME MEDALLION IS MADE
FROM GOLD SEAL AND SCRAPS OF RIBBON
OR PAPER.

hat is worn at a jaunty angle with one point forward and a feather on the side.

The Dutch girl's bonnet is made just like Robin Hood's, except that the corners are turned up and taped together to form flaps on the sides. This hat goes especially well with tulips and wooden shoes.

To make the Viking helmet:

(1) Cut a piece of newspaper approximately 23 inches square.

(2) Fold the paper diagonally as shown in figure 2.

(3) Fold corners B and D down so that they meet at A (figures 3 and 4).

(4) Fold corners B and D up so that they meet at E (figure 5).

(5) Fold corners B and D as shown in figures 6 and 7. The point at which they are folded should be about one third of the way down the sides of the square.

(6) Fold up the bottom corner A as shown in figure 8.

(7) Fold the front flap once more to form figure 9.

(8) Turn the paper over (figure 10) and fold the bottom corner up to meet the top point (figure 11). Tape everything in place, turn the paper over again, and you have a Viking helmet (figure 12).

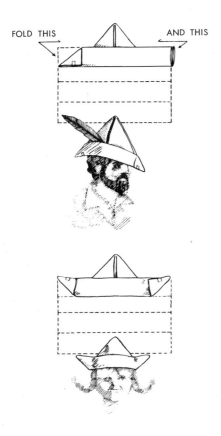

FOLD THIS　　　AND THIS

DUTCH GIRL'S BONNET.

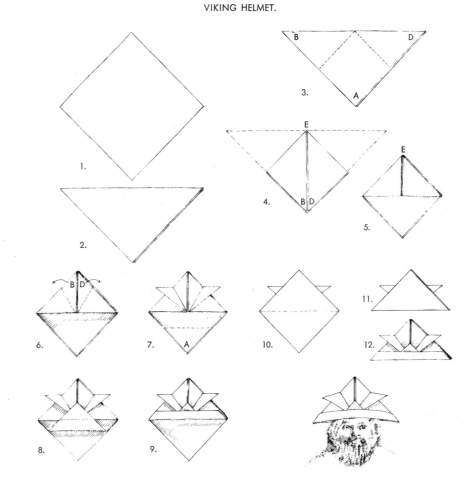

Terrible Pterodactyl

Far back in pre-history, in the period called the Mesozoic Era, the world was dominated by strange reptilian beasts. Dinosaurs roamed across the land, and plesiosaurs and ichthyosaurs inhabited the sea. The weirdest creature of all, however, had his kingdom in the air. He was the terrible pterodactyl, the winged menace, ruler of the skies. He measured 18 feet across his wings; and nobody smart would get in his way.

An encyclopedia will tell you that the pterodactyl (pronounced TARE-UH-<u>DAK</u>-TIL) is extinct. Unfortunately, this is not altogether true. He can be brought back to life all too easily by making the paper folds shown on these pages. But think twice. His manners are no better now than they were in the Mesozoic Era, and he will eat anything, even your fingers, if you aren't careful. Worst of all, he delights in attacking tin-can castles like the one on page 110 and stealing whatever he can carry off.

You'd be wise not to resurrect him, but if you feel you must:

(1) Take a square piece of paper and fold it

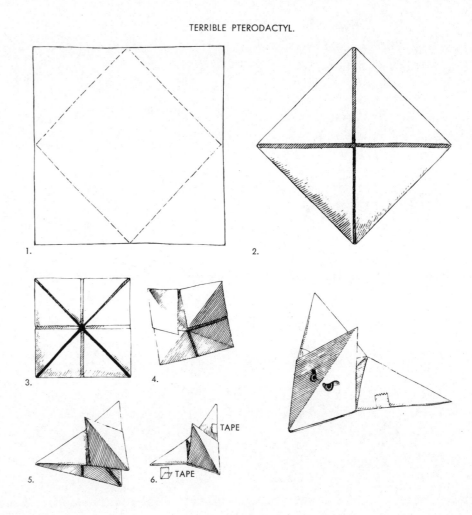

twice diagonally. Reopen the paper.
(2) Fold each corner into the center along the
dotted lines shown in figure 1 to form figure 2.
(3) Turn the paper over and fold each corner
into the center to form figure 3.
(4) Turn the paper over again, and pull one of
the corner folds forward (figure 4).
(5) Fold the opposite corner of the square under to
meet the corner you have pulled forward (figure 5).
Tape the sides together as shown (figure 6).
When you push the sides toward each
other, the middle part will snap open and closed
like a mouth. Yep, it's the terrible pterodactyl,
all right. All he needs now are some nasty looking
eyes, and he'll be off to create a nuisance
somewhere. You see? A real pest!

Paper Plane

Wherever you find paper, you'll find it being
folded into wings that soar and swoop and loop
through the air. These miniature planes float
out of New York office buildings; they sail over
small-town football fields. They're everywhere.
You've probably flown dozens of
models yourself, but here are two more you may
not have tried. The Swan is noted for long, gentle
sweeps through the air, while the Jay Bird wins
praise for its snappy aerial acrobatics. Try making
them from sheets of paper you find in the trash
basket rather than using up new sheets.
The Swan is a combination of two
airplanes. It begins with the classic paper flier
that almost everyone knows how to make:
(1) Fold an 8½ x 11-inch sheet of paper in half
lengthwise and unfold it again (figure 1).
(2) Fold the bottom corners up into the center
line (figure 2).
(3) Fold the diagonal sides into the center line
again (figure 3).
(4) Now turn it over (figure 4) and fold each

diagonal edge into the center line once again to form figure 5.

(5) Fold back on the center line, then turn the airplane over. Open out the wings and tape them together as shown.

To turn this into the Swan, you'll have to build another plane and attach it to the first. Take a second 8½ x 11-inch sheet of paper and fold it as above, through step 3.

(6) Slip the first plane into the second as shown in figure 6 and tape the two sections together. The Swan flies best if launched with a long, easy movement of the hand.

The Jay Bird is made in the following manner:

(1) Fold up the lower corner of an 8½ x 11-inch sheet of paper to form figure 1.

(2) Fold up the other corner to form figure 2.

(3) Unfold the paper, then fold it up horizontally at the point where the two diagonal creases meet (figure 3).

(4) Reopen the paper and push in the sides to form figure 4.

(5) Fold down the side flaps to form figure 5. They should not meet at the center.

(6) Fold up the bottom corner (figure 6).

(7) Fold the paper in half to form figure 7.

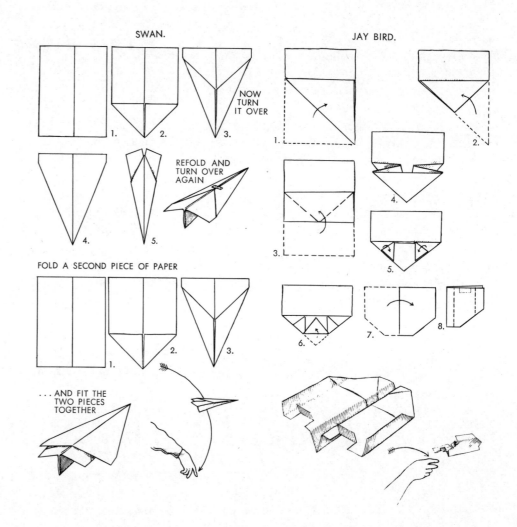

SWAN.

NOW TURN IT OVER

REFOLD AND TURN OVER AGAIN

FOLD A SECOND PIECE OF PAPER

...AND FIT THE TWO PIECES TOGETHER

JAY BIRD.

(8) Fold the sides back down about ¾ of an inch from the center crease to form the wings of the plane. Make a diagonal fold in each wing and turn the sides up slightly. Make two cuts in the rear of each wing and bend them up for tail flaps. (See the dotted lines in figure 8 for these three movements.)

The Jay Bird flies best when launched with a quick snap of the wrist.

No airplane is perfect, and no doubt you can improve upon these designs. Perhaps you could add a paper clip to the nose of the Jay Bird to give it more forward thrust, or you could pour a little glue into the point of the Swan to strengthen its tip. Maybe you could try bending all the stabilizer flaps down instead of up, just to see what happens. Experiment. After all, you're the aeronautical engineer.

Huge, closed rooms, where there are no drafts or air currents, are the best places for flying paper planes. But since these spaces are pretty hard to come by, you'll probably be launching your planes out of doors. Choose a still, calm day so that each model can show off its individual characteristics without too much interference from the wind.

And why not build a jetport for your fleet? It can be big and sprawling, with an air terminal made from paperboard boxes and rounded hangers built out of flexible corrugated paper. When you finish, airline symbols can be cut out of magazines and pasted on the top of each hanger.

Now you've got everything you need for exploring the skies. Almost. Don't forget your parachute. You'll find one on page 65.

Papier-Mâché Puppet

Papier-mâché has been used for many centuries, first by the Chinese and later by the Persians and Japanese. This mixture of paper pulp and glue was ideal for making masks and other festival objects. But its use was not limited to decorative items. In seventeenth-century France, for example, it was even used to make furniture. And the French gave it its name: papier, meaning paper, and mâché, meaning to reduce to pulp, which is what happens to the paper when it is soaked in water and mixed with glue.

Papier-mâché is an excellent material for constructing toy figures. It is especially good for making the heads for hand puppets. And of course it's a fine way to make use of waste paper.

There are several ways to make a papier-mâché puppet head, but this is the simplest method. Begin with a piece of Styrofoam or clay that is approximately the shape of the head you want. This will be the form over which you . will mold the papier-mâché. Make a hole in its underside for your finger to fit in later on. You can also use the shell of a soft-boiled egg as a

form for the puppet head. Open the egg carefully with an egg scissors or a sharp knife by slicing off just the pointed end. Empty out the egg with a small spoon, leaving the shell intact. Stuff the shell with a little cotton to prevent it from breaking.

You'll need something to hold the head steady while you work on it. Slip it onto the neck of a small Coke bottle or make a stand for it out of a wire coat hanger.

To make the coat-hanger stand, first press the hook of a wire hanger together so it can fit inside the eggshell. Then grasp the hook in one hand and the center of the bottom bar of the hanger in the other and pull them apart until the hanger is diamond-shaped. Finally, bend the bottom half of the diamond back to form a base. The hanger will now stand on its own. Wrap the hook in cotton by putting a piece through the center and folding it around the wire. Then insert it into the eggshell. Now you're ready to begin.

Using a ruler, tear newsprint into many strips about ½ inch wide by 6 inches long. Take a white emulsion glue, such as Elmer's, Sobo, or Wil-hold, and dilute it until it is a mixture of three parts water to one part glue. One quarter of a cup of glue and three quarters of a cup of water will make enough papier-mâché for two or three heads.

Now dip a strip of paper into the diluted glue, squeeze it out so it won't be too drippy, and apply it to the base form. Continue applying the glue-soaked strips to the form until you have covered it with approximately three layers of paper. You will need about twenty strips of newsprint. It is not necessary to let one layer dry before beginning the next.

As you apply the paper to the face, you will want to bunch it up to make a nose and ears and press it in to make a mouth and eyes. You can also dip string in the glue and work it into the papier-mâché to create special effects: eyebrows, wrinkles, hair, a mustache, ears, etc. Or you can add features made from bits of select garbage: tea leaves for eyebrows, grape seeds for eyes, elbow-macaroni for ears. If the papier-mâché isn't wet enough to hold these in place, use a bit of undiluted glue.

After the layering is complete, let the head stand until it is dry. You can set it near a radiator to speed up the drying, but even so, count on it taking a day to dry completely.

When the head is dry, it should be sealed. This can be done by brushing on three coats of undiluted white glue. Let the head dry after each coat. When it is sealed, you can lift it off the stand, carefully removing any cotton that has stuck to it. If you want a smooth finish, sand the last coats with very fine sandpaper.

Now the puppet is ready to perform— almost. He'll need some clothes, of course. You can cut out a coat like the one in the drawing, then sew the sides together, leaving the top and bottom open. Sew the neck of the coat to the neck of the papier-mâché head. Insert your hand through the bottom of the coat, put a finger in each arm and one or two up through the top hole into the head. Wiggle your fingers to make the puppet move.

An even simpler costume can be made from a old pillowcase. Cut off one corner of the pillowcase diagonally, then place your index and center fingers together in the closed corner of the triangle, and insert them into the egghead. Use your thumb and little finger for the puppet's arms.

You can make a puppet theater by cutting a stage opening in one side of a large corrugated box. Slide a curtain across it, and you're in show business.

What about a play? Well, you don't

have to follow a real script. You can even write
your own. If you get a chance to see some
"professional" puppet theater, go and borrow
a few ideas from them. Or make characters to
represent yourself and your friends and use them
to play as you might yourselves. Or act out
your favorite story, even using a few lines
of dialogue directly from the book. If you are
very enterprising, you can produce a real play.
Your library will have books full of them and
the librarian will be glad to help you select one.
But try to pick one that doesn't have too many
characters, or you'll never finish getting ready
for the show!

PAPERBOARD

More containers and packages are made from paperboard than from any other material. This isn't surprising when you realize that "paperboard" includes ordinary pasteboard, cardboard, corrugated cardboard, and fiberboard. It can be seen in every store in a variety of forms: shipping boxes, cereal packages, ice-cream cartons, paper-towel tubes, display racks. Paperboard is popular because it is strong, light, and inexpensive.

Like paper, paperboard begins in the forest. A tree is cut down and turned into wood pulp, which is then mixed and beaten and rolled and layered into paperboard. Paperboard can also be made from recycled material. Some paperboard boxes, for example, are gray on their unprinted sides because they are made from waste paper that has not been de-inked. During the manufacturing process, the ink stamping from old packages merges with the new paperboard, turning it a smudgy color.

Though paperboard can be made from used material, very little is. In fact less recycled board is produced today than ten years ago. This is not because there's not enough waste paper and used paperboard available for reclamation. There's plenty for today and for the future. It is because the public has not demonstrated to the manufacturers its desire for recycled board.

The wide use of paperboard makes it, along with paper, the largest part of the solid wastes generated by our cities. Luckily, it is relatively easy to get rid of by crushing or burning. And it is biodegradable, which means that when left outdoors in the sun, rain, and snow, it will rot down to become part of the soil. Other biodegradable packaging materials are paper, wood, and cloth. Some metals eventually rust and return to the soil, but plastics and glass are firmly nondegradable.

So paperboard could be an ideal material. It makes a good, strong package; it can be recycled; and it can be disposed of readily. Perhaps best of all, it makes terrific homemade toys and games. It's easy to cut and glue, and there's plenty of it to choose from.

Paperboard Periscope

Are you not quite tall enough to watch the ball game over the fence? Do people stand in front of you at parades? Well, your troubles are over. Now, thanks to a paperboard tube, you can peer over any kind of obstacle that gets in your way.

To build this periscope you'll need a paperboard tube approximately 20 inches in length and 1½ inches in diameter, with good thick walls. If you can't locate the perfect tube, you can tape together two paper-towel tubes. You will also need a 7-inch length of broomstick, which you can saw off from the rest of the handle, and two small mirrors.

(1) To begin, cut the 7-inch length of handle at a 45-degree angle, about 1 inch from one end. You now have two pieces of wood, one shorter, one longer, both with one slanted end (figure 1).

(2) Glue a small pocket mirror on the slanted face of each piece of wood as shown in figure 2.

(3) Now take the cardboard tube and cut a 1-inch square out of opposite ends as shown in figure 3.

(4) The two pieces of wood must fit snugly inside

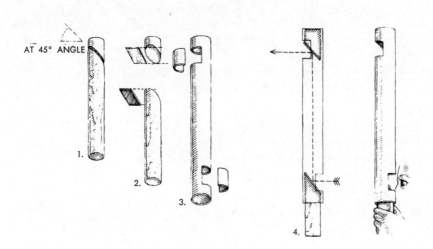

AT 45° ANGLE

1.

2.

3.

4.

either end of the tube. If the diameter of the wood is smaller than that of the tube, you can build up the wood by wrapping a strip of corrugated cardboard around each piece just below the mirror. Then fit the longer piece of broom handle into the bottom of the tube to form a handle for your periscope (figure 4). Make sure the mirror faces the opening you cut in the wall of the tube. Fit the shorter piece into the top of the tube, again with the mirror facing the opening. Glue both pieces of wood securely into place.

Cover the tube with aluminum foil or paint it with enamel or varnish to help protect it from moisture.

Now hold your completed periscope by the wooden handle and bring it up to your eye. The action of the mirrors makes it possible to look in the lower window but actually see out the upper one. At last, an unobstructed view!

Egg-Carton Caterpillar

This zoological wonder is made from a molded-pulp egg carton, some colored pipe cleaners, and two buttons.

Begin by cutting one row of egg pockets free from the bottom of the carton with a knife. Trim the row so that each pocket is cleanly rounded and lay it on a flat surface with the open side down. Bend two pipe cleaners of the same color into a pair of antennae and push them into holes in the top of the first section. Glue two button eyes on the sides, draw on a mouth, and the head is complete.

Each remaining section of the body will now require two legs. Select a pipe cleaner of a color different from the antennae, bend it to a suitable shape, and use it as a model for all the rest. You should make the legs long enough so that the end pushed through the carton can be bent under and glued in place. Finally, add a pipe-cleaner tail that matches the antennae in color.

Strange fellow, isn't he? Just about as strange as the caterpillar that Alice encountered during her adventures in Wonderland, the one that sat on a mushroom all day long, smoking a hookah pipe. Alice, herself, and other characters from Wonderland can be found on pages 61, 62, and 63.

Boxville, U.S.A.

If you look carefully at the streets of the town you live in, you will see that most of the buildings are combinations of simple geometric forms: cubes, cylinders, pyramids. Paperboard packages with these same geometric shapes can be used to reproduce your town in miniature.

To become a city planner for a while, you'll need lots of boxes of all different sizes, plus egg cartons, cardboard tubes, matchboxes, and milk cartons.

One way to begin is to get a head-on photograph or drawing of the streets you want to re-create. Then mark up the pictures to show the basic geometric shapes of the buildings. Find packages of the same shapes to represent the buildings. You may have to combine several boxes to make one building if it is not a simple form. Of course, you can work from real life, too. Just look at the buildings and decide which packages would best represent them.

Once you have selected the packages, work with them to reproduce as exactly as possible the front of each building. Cut windows and doors in the front, then hang clear plastic wrapping paper inside the box to make windowpanes. Extra boxes can be cut in half diagonally to make sloping roofs; egg-carton sections can be used for domes; half-round cheese boxes can be glued on for theatre marquees. Use interlocking plastic ice-cream sticks, such as those made by The Borden Company, for fire escapes and lattices. Toilet-paper rolls are fine for columns. The corners of plastic berry boxes make perfect balconies.

You can use paint, colored tape, or wrapping paper to decorate the buildings. Or you can pick boxes with interesting designs and leave them as they are. Finally, use dry noodles and spaghetti for architectural details such as moldings, ledges, etc.

Now line up the buildings to make a street. As you add buildings, you can make more streets, and finally a whole town. Improve upon your home town by arranging the city in such a way as to prevent traffic jams, facilitate garbage collection, and provide plenty of space for parks and gardens.

Paperboard Pyramids

When Hernando Cortes came to Mexico in 1519, he discovered deep inside the country a beautiful island city called Tenochtitlan (TE-NOTCH-TI-TLAN). It was the capital of the Aztec Empire, and Montezuma was its emperor. The city, with its gleaming pyramids and sun-struck monuments, seemed like the legendary City of Gold to Cortes and his men. In spite of their admiration for it, the Spaniards destroyed Tenochtitlan when they captured it, and built Mexico City in its place.

If you'd like to try being an archeologist, you can reconstruct the ancient Aztec capital out of paperboard boxes, just as you did your own home town (page 48).

The center of Tenochtitlan was the ceremonial plaza, where the pyramids stood. The grandest of these terraced monuments was dedicated to the two chief gods of the Aztecs, the Sun God and the Rain God. Aztec divinities had wonderfully unpronounceable names, and these two were no exceptions: Huitzilopochtli, the Sun God, pronounced WEET-ZEEL-O-POTCH-TLY;

and Tlaloc, the Rain God, pronounced <u>TLAH</u>-LOC. Don't worry. Cortes and his men couldn't pronounce them either!

Aztec pyramids were quite different from Egyptian ones, although certain archeologists think there may be some still-undiscovered link between them. Egyptian pyramids, of course, were the tombs of the pharoahs, with slanted sides and secret burial chambers inside. Their Mexican counterparts, however, were built to honor the gods, and their interiors were solid, with no hidden rooms. Their sides were composed of a series of stone terraces which served as a symbolic stairway to heaven. On the highest level of each pyramid there was always a temple which in the minds of the people was the dwelling place of the god to whom that pyramid was dedicated.

To make the pyramid of Tlaloc and Huitzilopochtli and the other monuments and palaces that stood in the center of the city, begin piling your boxes on top of one another, closed sides up. Start with the largest ones on the bottom and build to the smallest ones on top. Shuffle them around until you have several pyramids of different sizes. You may have to cut down some of the boxes to keep the changes in level from being too abrupt. When you're satisfied, glue the various pieces together.

You can make a temple for the top of each pyramid by laying a closed egg carton across two cardboard-tube columns, as shown in the drawing. Build a flight of steps leading up to the temple out of staggered match boxes. At the center of the temple, place a large plastic cap for use as an altar.

Houses for the city can be made from empty milk cartons. Wash them out carefully and reseal their tops with glue. Hold the tops in place with a paper clip until the glue is dry. With a knife cut the cartons into two parts, horizontally, varying the size of the segments so that you will have both one- and two-story structures. The tops of the cartons make houses with pitched roofs, and the bottoms make houses with flat roofs. Cut out openings in the sides for windows and doorways.

Now arrange your large buildings around the open plaza. The biggest pyramid should stand alone at one end, dominating the entire city. Emperor Montezuma's palace should stand to one side of the pyramid. The milk-carton houses can be used to form smaller plazas leading off from the main square.

There were many secret rooms within the Emperor's palace. One of these was Montezuma's treasure chamber, where his enormous fortune was hidden. You can re-create this astonishing room by lining the inside of a cigar box with gold paper and filling it with old gold buttons and gleaming jewels and silver chains. Close it and stand it against the side of Montezuma's palace with the front side facing out and the hinged edge at the bottom. To Cortes it will look like just another level of the palace, but when you touch the secret lock, the front panel will fall forward to reveal the greatest treasure in the New World.

Of course not all the wealth of Tenochtitlan was hidden. Much of it was used to decorate the buildings of the city. You can enrich your buildings by painting them with poster paints. White walls with orange and blue borders were used by the Aztecs. If the milk-carton houses have a wax coating, they won't accept paint, so cover them with paper instead. Add bands of Indian motifs around the terraces of the pyramids and cover the columns of the temples with gold foil. On the front of Montezuma's palace, paint an eagle holding a serpent in its claw, the proud symbol of Tenochtitlan.

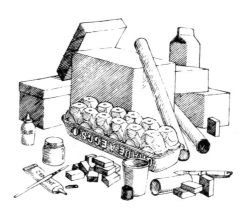

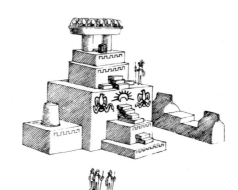

To people your city, make the clothespin characters described on page 23. You can use red pipe-cleaner arms for the Aztecs and yellow for the Spaniards. Montezuma can have an elaborate headdress made from a gold button and paper feathers, while Cortes can wear a silver helmet made from aluminum foil.

The encyclopedia will tell you the whole history of the emperor and the conquistador. You'll find out how Cortes used treachery to kidnap Montezuma, how the Spaniards were almost wiped out on the Sad Night, and how they finally came back and captured the city.

Aztec Idol

The Aztec city of Tenochtitlan was filled with huge pieces of sculpture before the Spaniards came. There were great stone idols everywhere. They were carved with the terrible features of Tlaloc and Huitzilopochtli and the other fearsome gods of the Indians. You can make these idols for the Aztec city on page 49 by using corrugated paper and glue.

Corrugated paper comes in various forms, but the kind you will need is composed of a layer of flat paper and a layer of fluted paper. This combination creates a strong, flexible cushion, which can be used to protect objects that are being shipped. You can find it inside discarded packing crates or you can buy rolls of it in department stores.

To make an Aztec idol, start with a round paperboard box, for example, a Quaker Oats container. Glue a layer of corrugated paper around it, with the fluted side out. Now glue on more and more pieces of corrugated paper to form a headdress, ears, and scowling features. By building up layers, by making loops, by forming bulges, you can quickly create an awe-inspiring pagan god.

The drawing will give you an idea of what can be done. But don't try to copy it. Make up a better sculpture of your own. And be ready to take advantage of any accidents that happen, like cutting a piece too short or gluing an ear on upside down. Accidents are often where new ideas begin.

When the head is finished, make a neck from a ring of corrugated paper to provide a base for the idol. Paint the strange deity in wild pagan colors and set it up high on one of your buildings, where it can scare the daylights out of the clothespin Spaniards below.

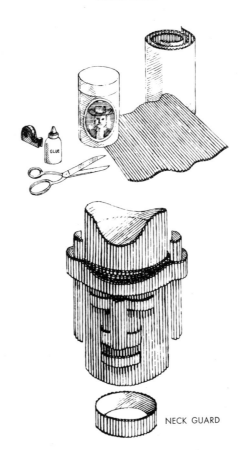

NECK GUARD

Corrugated Paper Helmet

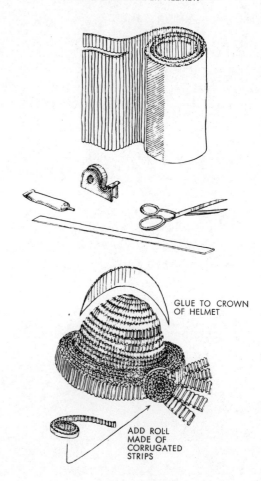

GLUE TO CROWN OF HELMET

ADD ROLL MADE OF CORRUGATED STRIPS

While you're building the Aztec city on page 49, you may want to wear the helmet of Montezuma or Cortes. You can make these helmets and many others from one single piece of corrugated paper. Just cut long strips of the paper, 1½ inches in width. Tape their ends together, and wind them tightly in one big roll. Glue the end of the last strip to the piece beneath it to hold the roll together.

Now gently push on the center of the roll until the strips begin to move out and form a cone. Push the strips in or out until you have a helmet that you like. Wear it for a while and later flatten the whole thing out and make another design.

If you want to make a design permanent, apply spots of glue to the underside of each strip to hold it in place. After a hat has been glued, it can be painted.

Montezuma's headdress can be decorated with Ping-pong balls and feathers and

plastic bottle caps so he can impress his people.
Cortes and his soldiers, on the other hand, will
wear their helmets primarily for military purposes,
so you may want to add to the Spanish hats
the neckguard shown in the drawing.

Helmets are not the only thing you
can make with your corrugated-paper roll. How
about a base for an Aztec monument? Or a
roulette wheel for marbles? Or a volcano? Push
and pull a little. There's no telling what you'll
come up with.

CLOTH AND STRING

Try to imagine a world without cloth.
To begin with, you'd be naked, or "clothed" perhaps in garments made of paper. There would be no fabrics on the furniture, no rugs on the floors, no blankets on the beds. It would not be impossible to get along, but much of the richness, beauty, and comfort of our lives would be lost.

Cloth is so important to us that it has become a metaphor for civilization. We speak of the "fabric of society," or the way in which separate individuals, like separate threads, weave together to create a larger community. The ancient Greeks and Romans represented Fate as three goddesses who wove the cloth of human destiny on their spinning wheels.

Cloth comes from many sources: wool and silk from animals, cotton and linen from plants, and man-made fibers such as nylon and rayon from the chemical laboratory. Man-made fibers were only developed in this century, but linen was being made from the flax plant as far back as 3000 B.C. And the Chinese were raising silkworms in 2640 B.C.

For many centuries cloth was made in the home by women who spun and wove yarn into fabrics. In the eighteenth century, the Industrial Revolution removed textile manufacturing to factories, where power-driven machinery could do much of the work. Yet labor conditions in these factories were almost unbearable: men, women, and children worked endless hours in filthy, dark, airless rooms, for penny wages. It was many years before unions and labor laws could improve conditions for factory workers.

Today cloth is used very little in packaging, usually only for feed and seed, so you won't find much of it in the supermarket. You will find a lot of used cloth in the home, though, especially in the form of old clothes. You can use the clothing to make costumes and masks and flags, of course, but if it is still wearable, try passing it along to someone who needs it. This is cloth recycling at its best.

When cloth is so worn out that it can't even be used to make toys, it still has value. Both cloth and string can be recycled into paper. The finest papers, in fact, are made from these materials. And paper manufacturers are very proud of the rag content of their products.

String has been used by man even longer than cloth has. Since it is made by simply twisting fibers or strands together, even the earliest civilizations used it in the form of rope to control their animals, rig their ships, drag their building materials to construction sites.

One of the earliest industries in this country was a "rope-walk" established in Boston in 1642. Workers twisted fibers together into rope by walking back and forth in a long room. This slow hand technique continued to be used until machines for making rope and string were developed about 1820.

Cloth and string are so familiar to us that it's sometimes hard to remember to save them for making toys and games. Tie a string around your finger so you won't forget.

Patchwork

For the early settlers of the United States, cloth was a rare and valuable item. It had to be brought over from Europe or woven by hand at home, so every spare piece was saved and used again, usually in making the colorful bed coverings called patchwork quilts.

The quilts were made by sewing small pieces of material together along their edges, either in a simple checkerboard pattern or in more complex designs with names like "Log Cabin," "Wedding Band," and "Crazy Quilt." Often the making of a quilt became a social event, a quilting bee, where neighbors would get together to work on the same quilt around a big wooden frame.

You can carry on this early example of recycling by making patchwork accessories for the crate houses on page 17. Save all the remnants you can find, and you'll be able to make miniature quilts, draperies, even a rug.

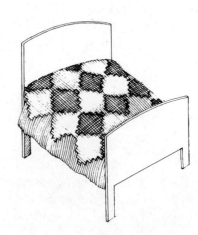

A small quilt can be made from 1-inch squares of cloth put together to form a 6 x 8-inch checkerboard pattern. First cut out all the squares with pinking shears so they won't ravel. You'll need 48 squares in all. Cut out another piece of material, 8 inches by 10 inches, and lay the small squares on it, leaving a 1-inch border all around the outside. Move the squares around until you have each one where you want it in the design. Light and dark pieces should alternate so that each patch will stand out clearly. You can also lay the squares out in a diagonal pattern, as shown in the drawing.

Now put a small amount of rubber cement under each patch to hold it in place. This isn't the way real patchwork quilts are made, of course, but it is a simple method for making miniature ones.

A slightly different system can be used to make a patchwork rug. Take a piece of cardboard the size and shape of the rug you want and glue cloth patches onto it using rubber cement. When all the pieces have been applied, trim the edges and glue the cardboard to the floor of the crate room you are decorating.

Raggedy Alice

"**C**uriouser and curiouser!" cried Alice. She had followed the White Rabbit down the rabbit hole, and now she was in a strange and marvelous land, where just about anything could happen. Why, she could drink from a bottle marked "DRINK ME" and shrink until she was only ten inches high. Or she could eat a cake marked "EAT ME" and grow and stretch until her head hit the ceiling. Yes, it was curious, but it wasn't impossible. Nothing was impossible in Wonderland. Lewis Carroll began writing Alice's Adventures in Wonderland in 1862. It has delighted everyone, old and young, ever since. By using throwaways, you can make the various characters that Alice encountered in her travels. The White Rabbit can be made from a square of cloth (page 64), the Queen of Hearts and Tweedle-Dum and Tweedle-Dee can be put together from plastic bottles (page 87), and the hookah-smoking Caterpillar can be fashioned from an egg carton (page 47). Alice herself, both big and small, can be made from remnants of cloth, a little cotton, and some yarn.

To make Alice when she was big, begin by drawing on tissue paper a simplified outline of her body a little larger than you want her to be. You'll find she shrinks a bit even as you make her. If you have trouble making each part of the body the right size, try marking squares on the tissue paper before drawing your pattern, then use them as a guide. For example, if the head is 2 squares from top to bottom, then the body should be about 2 squares from shoulder to waist, etc. You can follow the proportions shown in the drawing. Then choose a wide piece of unpatterned cloth to be her skin. Fold it in half to make two layers.

Use the paper outline as a pattern by pinning it to one side of the folded cloth and cutting around its edges through both layers of cloth. Unpin the pattern, then sew the two pieces of cloth together just as they are, around the edges, leaving openings at the top of the head and the end of each arm and leg, through which you can add the stuffing.

Now turn the cloth inside out and stuff it with kapok or cotton or small soft rags. The body can be stiff or floppy, depending on how much stuffing you add. If you want the knees and elbows to bend, make a row of stitches across

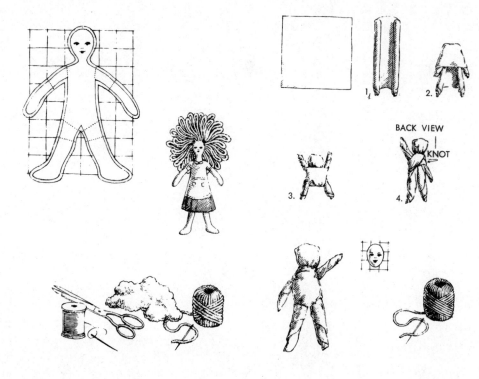

RAGGEDY ALICE WHEN SHE WAS BIG.

RAGGEDY ALICE WHEN SHE WAS LITTLE.

BACK VIEW

KNOT

1.
2.
3.
4.

the joints after each section has been stuffed. In order to do this, the sections must be stuffed and sewn off one by one, starting with the farthest parts of the legs and arms and working toward the body and the head. When you have finished, sew up the stuffing holes.

Now you can draw on Alice's face with a felt-tip pen or stitch on her mouth and eyes with a needle and thread. Add a light blue dress and a white apron and lots of yarn for hair.

The other Alice, Alice when she was tiny, can be made in only a couple of minutes, just about the time it took her to drink the bottle of magic liquid and shrink to the size of a mouse. You'll need only one piece of fairly thin cloth, the size and shape of a handkerchief.

(1) Lay out the cloth on a flat surface and roll up both sides, as shown in figure 1.

(2) At a point about one third of the way down the length of the cloth, make a fold and lay the upper part over the lower part, as in figure 2.

(3) Now fold the lower part up over the upper section (figure 3) and pull the ends of each roll out slightly to lengthen them. The ends pointing up will become the arms and the ends pointing down will become the legs.

(4) Pull the arms behind the upper bit of cloth, which becomes a head, and tie them in a simple knot (figure 4).

Do a little adjusting, a little pushing and pulling, and your throwaway rag will slowly turn into tiny Alice. Finally, paste on a drawing of Alice's face and add some yarn for hair.

Now you have Alice when she was big and Alice when she was small. But all these changes in size were a little upsetting for her. " 'It was much pleasanter at home,' thought poor Alice, 'when one wasn't always growing larger and smaller, and being ordered around by mice and rabbits. I almost wish I hadn't gone down that rabbit-hole, and yet, and yet—it's rather curious, you know, this sort of life. . . .' "

White Rabbit

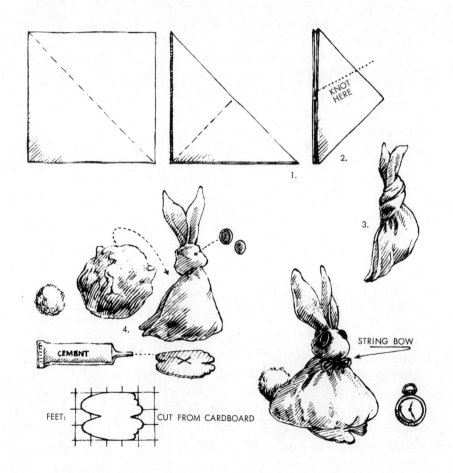

One of the creatures that Alice encounters in her adventures in Wonderland is the White Rabbit. He's the one who actually leads her to Wonderland in the first place. Like many of the characters she meets, though, he's just a little bit unpleasant. He's terribly nervous, always hurrying along, always checking his pocket watch, always complaining to himself, "Dear, dear! I shall be late!"

Luckily, you can make your own version of the White Rabbit in such a short time that even _he_ would be pleased. You'll need only two fairly thin pieces of cloth to do it, each about the size of a handkerchief.

(1) Take the first square of cloth and hold it by two opposite corners so that it makes a big triangle (figure 1).

(2) Put these two corners together to form a smaller triangle (figure 2).

(3) Tie a simple knot in the cloth about halfway down the side of the triangle, as shown by the dotted line in figure 2, and pull the two ends

through the knot to form figure 3. These ends are the rabbit's ears, and the knot is his head. (4) Push the rest of the cloth around until it becomes a kind of pocket. Stuff the other remnant into this pocket to form the body, and tuck in any leftover flaps (figure 4).

Cut out a cardboard base like the one in the drawing and glue it to the cloth. Glue on a puff of cotton for a tail and sew on buttons for eyes. And, of course, give him a little cardboard pocket watch. He musn't be late.

Cloth Parachute

The paper planes on page 35 are spectacular fliers, but, well, there's always the chance that a parachute will be needed. Just in case, here's how to make one.

First find a square of very thin cloth, about the size of a handkerchief. Locate its exact center by folding it twice diagonally. At this center point, draw a red dot about one quarter inch in diameter.

Tie a 1-foot length of string to each of the four corners of the square. Bring the free ends of the string together and tie them in a knot about three inches from the bottom. For a weight, tie on a metal washer or—and this is more fun— make a little cork parachutist like the one in the drawing and strap him in. He should be just about the right weight, but if not, give him a button backpack to make him heavier.

Pick up the parachute by the red dot, hold it as high in the air as you can, and let it drop. It will billow out and float your parachutist safely to the ground. Try dropping him from a

66.

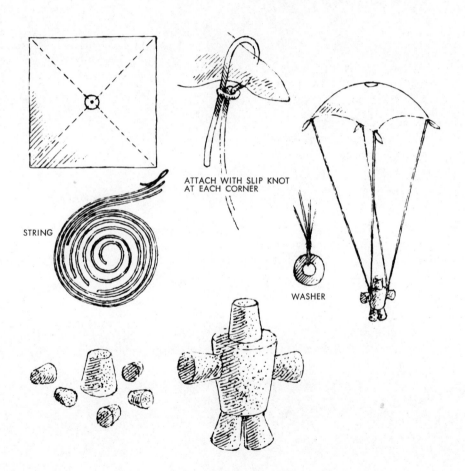

STRING

ATTACH WITH SLIP KNOT
AT EACH CORNER

WASHER

chair or over the side of the staircase. The higher you are, the longer his ride will be.

If your parachute begins to give you trouble, you might check to see if the lines are tangled. If that doesn't work, you might add more weight to the string. If _that_ doesn't work, you might try shouting "Geronimo!" before each jump. It's the traditional word used by jumpers to bring good luck. Geronimo was the chief of the Apache Indians, a man of great bravery and daring. If your parachutist is half as brave as Geronimo, you won't need to worry.

String Figures

People all over the world have enjoyed making string figures since before anyone can remember. By looping string over and around and between their fingers, they could make simple string drawings of animals, boats, trees. Through the centuries designs passed from friend to friend, from country to country, so that today even an Eskimo and an Australian, if given a loop of string, could find a common interest.

You probably know how to make several string figures, yourself. Experts know hundreds of figures and have special names to describe the movements used to create them. But you won't need any special training to make the figures explained here. All you'll need is a piece of smooth, fairly thick string, about 6½ feet long, knotted together to form a continuous loop.

The first figure is called Man Climbing a Tree, and it comes from the back country of eastern Australia. It is made by carrying out the following steps, which are not as complicated as they sound:

(1) Begin with the string looped over the thumb

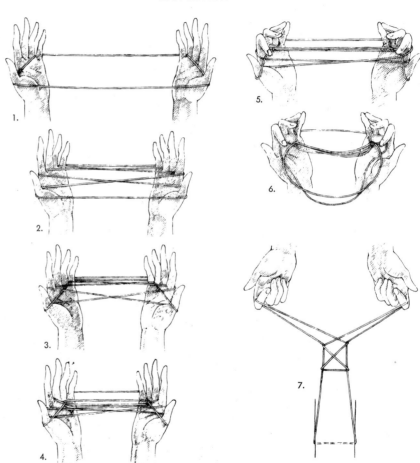

CROW'S FEET.

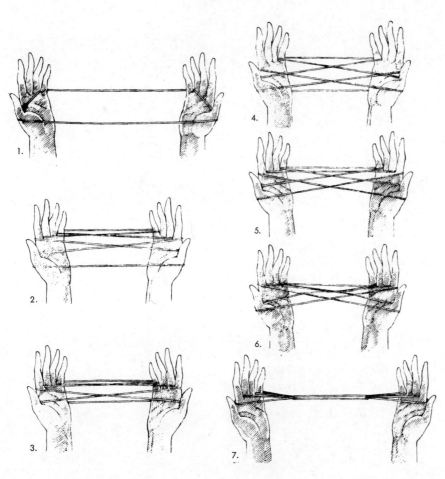

1.

2.

3.

4.

5.

6.

7.

and little finger of each hand, as shown in figure 1. (2) Pass the index finger of the right hand under the string lying across the palm of the left hand and pull it tight. Repeat the action with the left index finger. This is known in string-figure terminology as "Opening A" (figure 2).

(3) Bend each little finger across the strings toward your body. With the back of each little finger, pick up the string nearest you and move the finger back to its original position. The string should still remain looped around the thumbs, but there are now two loops around each little finger as well (figure 3).

(4) Using your left hand, pick up the bottom loop on the right little finger, pass it over the upper loop, and slip it over the top of the finger to free it. Repeat for the left little finger (figure 4). This is called "Navahoing the loop," because this movement, which is used all over the world, was first discovered among the Navaho Indians.

(5) Bend each index finger down over the string that crosses the finger at its base and press fingertips into the palm of your hand (figure 5). The strings that pass across each palm will then be locked in by the index fingers.

(6) Hold the strings loosely and slip the loops off the thumbs. Keeping the tips of your index fingers

on your palms, separate your hands and let the loops on your index fingers slip off (figure 6).
(7) Finally, slip the far string on the little fingers under a heavy book or under your foot and release the little fingers. Keep index fingers hooked into the loops they hold and pull gently. The outlines of a towering tree trunk will appear, and as you continue to pull, a little string man with arms and legs crossed around the trunk will scramble up its entire length.

The second pattern is the most widely known of all string figures. The Cherokee Indians call it Crow's Feet, although there are many other names for it. It has been found in places as far apart as Africa, Australia, America, and the Pacific Islands.

It is constructed in the following manner:
(1) Begin with the string looped over the thumb and little finger of each hand just as you did in Man Climbing a Tree (figure 1).
(2) Carry out Opening A by picking the palm strings up by the back of your index fingers, then separating your hands (figure 2).
(3) Close the fingers of each hand and insert them from above into the loop nearest you, the thumb loop. With your fingers still closed, throw the string nearest you over the backs of your hands to the far side. Open your fingers once more to form figure 3.
(4) Transfer each index-finger loop to the thumb of the same hand (figure 4).
(5) Transfer the loop on the back of each hand to the index finger of that hand (figure 5).
(6) Take the near little-finger string on each hand and pass it through the index-finger loop from below. Place it on the far side of your little finger, and Navaho the lower little-finger loop; that is, move it past the upper loop and off the finger.
(7) Release the thumb loops and pull your hands apart. This is the moment of truth. If you've done each step correctly, a large set of crow's feet will suddenly appear.

You'll find that each time you try them, string figures become easier. But be careful or you'll end up spending all your free time with a loop of string.

String Guillotine

The French have used a machine called the guillotine for chopping off the heads of those who were sentenced to death. It was officially adopted for use in all executions just before the French Revolution. It was named after Joseph Ignace Guillotin, a doctor of the time who advocated its use as a quick, humane method of capital punishment. Dr. Guillotin was hoping to alleviate suffering, and he had no idea that his name, by association with the death device, would become one of the most feared words in the French language.

By using string, you can do a trick called The Guillotine, in which you will appear to cut your own throat. You'll actually be performing a slight-of-hand, which means you'll be moving your hands so quickly and surely that any onlooker will be deceived.

(1) Stretch a loop of string between your thumbs and let its middle part rest against the back of your neck, as in figure 1. Tell a gullible friend that you are about to make the string pass completely through your neck, like the blade of a guillotine.

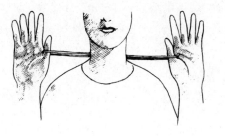

1.

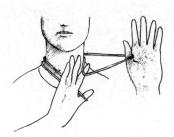

2.

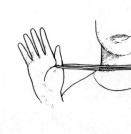

3.

4.

(2) Then slip your right index finger into the loop
held by your left thumb and pull (figure 2). At
the same time, release the loop on your right thumb.
(3) As the string is sliding around your neck,
slip the right loop from your index finger back
onto your thumb (figure 3).
(4) When you are once again holding the string
in front of you on both thumbs, it will look as if it
has actually passed through your neck (figure 4).
        The whole action must be carried out
with lightening speed if it is to appear convincing.
Additional shock value can be gained by uttering
a choked gurgle and crossing your eyes as the
imaginary blade slices through your vocal cords.

GLASS

The first glass was made not by man, but by nature. Long before man appeared on earth, glass was formed whenever lightning struck a mixture of sand, limestone, and soda ash. These materials melted together, leaving a thin glaze on the surface of the earth or long roots of glass that penetrated deep into the ground. The heat of volcanic fires and molten lava could do the same thing.

Cave dwellers used this form of glass, which is called obsidian, to make knives and arrowheads. It is not known exactly how or when man learned to make glass for himself. Pliny, a Roman historian, claimed that the secret was discovered by accident. According to him, the crew of a Phoenician trading ship built a small fire on a sandy beach one night. They used chunks of soda ash, the cargo they were carrying, to support their cooking utensils. When they finished cooking and the fire cooled, the men found a hard, glittering material in the ashes. The heat of the flames had melted sand and soda ash together to form glass.

Making containers from glass was very difficult in the early days. Workmen had to pull fine strands of molten glass out of a vat, then wind these strands little by little around a mold made of sand. About 300 B.C., however, the blowpipe was discovered. Someone found that a glass bubble could be made by blowing very hard through a pipe that had a glob of molten glass on one end. Then, by rotating the pipe as the glass cooled, the bubble could be fashioned into a container. It was a big step forward.

Today the ingredients of glass are heated together in a huge furnace at temperatures as high as 2700 degrees Fahrenheit. A glass-blowing machine picks up a small glob of molten glass, places it in a mold, and blows compressed air through it to create a bubble within the mold. When the mold opens, there is the finished bottle. The whole process, from glob to bottle, takes only about thirteen seconds.

Glass containers are much easier to make today than centuries ago, but they are no less useful. They will not rust, rot, decay, or burn; they are transparent, moisture-proof, sanitary, and odorless; and they can be refilled over and over again. In addition, they can be recycled—crushed down into "cullet," which is used in the manufacture of new glass.

The bad thing about a glass bottle, of course, is that it can break. When carelessly tossed aside as litter, it becomes a real danger.

Glass fragments from a broken bottle or jar can cut people, animals, tires. It's much safer and much more fun to recycle bottles into toys and games.

Bottle Garden

If you'd like to see what a pure natural environment is like, one that isn't polluted, one that completely recycles its resources, then plant a garden in a bottle. You'll have a miniature version of what our own environment once was. Better, you'll be able to study what our surroundings can be again when we learn to control the impurities that we pour into them.

The first requirement for your garden is a big bottle, a really big one, with a fairly large mouth that can be easily corked or sealed in some manner. Old-fashioned water jugs or five-gallon pickle jars are fine. If you don't have one in the basement, you can usually find them at junk shops or flea markets. Wash your bottle well in hot water and disinfectant and remove any stains by soaking it overnight in a strong solution of laundry bleach.

For tools you'll need a long wooden stick with a point at one end and a wire clothes hanger that has been bent into a pruning hook. To pour the soil into the jug, you'll need a funnel, which can be made from the neck of a plastic bottle.

You'll also need some good, rich, sterilized soil and a box of uncolored aquarium gravel, both of which can be bought at the dime store. Finally, you'll need several small pieces of charcoal and a large cork.

Begin by pouring a small amount of aquarium gravel through the plastic funnel and into the bottle, just enough to form a 1-inch layer on the bottom to aid in drainage. Pour at least two inches of soil on top of the gravel, enough to fill the lower quarter of the bottle. Spread it out evenly with the wooden stick and drop in a few small pieces of charcoal to prevent the soil from smelling sour.

You're now ready to plant. Choosing the right plants is important. You'll want ones that have similar growing needs and aren't too large for the bottle. Miniature ferns and other small plants that like shade and moisture are best. Small-leaved English ivy, prayer plants, maidenhair fern, and small palms are all good choices. You'll want to select plants that form an interesting landscape, with contrasting leaf patterns and varying shades of green. You won't need very many—after all, your garden is quite small, and plants need room to grow.

Decide on the arrangement of your plants before you put them in the bottle. If the bottle garden is to be seen from one side only, place the taller plants toward the back; if it is to be seen from all sides, put the taller plants in the middle and the shorter ones around the outside. After you've decided on the layout, use the pointed end of the stick to form a planting hole for each plant. Carefully slip each plant through the opening into the bottle. Then push its roots into the hole. Use the blunt end of the stick to push the soil in around the roots, covering them well. If you're good with chopsticks, you'll probably find this easy to do. If not, you won't. But don't worry about mistakes. Just pull the plant up and try again.

Some of the plants may not stand erect when they are first put in place. You can prop them up with pebbles or lean them against their neighbors. Leave some open spaces between the plants and landscape these with moss and small, unusual pieces of wood.

Use the coat-hanger pruning hook to make any final arrangements. If there are dirt smudges on the inside of the glass, cover the hook with paper toweling and use it to wipe them off.

Finally, sprinkle the soil with just

enough water to moisten it evenly. Cork the bottle tightly and place it in a bright place that never receives direct sunlight. You now have a completely self-sufficient garden, and it should require no further maintenance except occasional pruning. It needs no watering because nature will recycle the existing moisture for use again and again.

This is called the hydrologic cycle. You'll be able to watch it in action: light and heat will evaporate the ground wetness, which will then rise as vapor and condense on the inside of the glass into beads of moisture. At the same time, the plants will be taking water from the soil and, through transpiration, turning it into vapor, which will also condense on the glass. Later on, the beads of moisture on the bottle will drop like rain to water the plants and start the cycle all over again.

If no beads of moisture appear on the bottle, it means that there was not enough water in your garden to begin with or that the cork is loose. Add a small amount of water and recork the bottle. If the glass is always cloudy, there is too much water in the bottle. Remove the cork and allow the interior to dry out until the glass clears. Then recork the bottle.

You'll find that plants turn their leaves in the direction of the sun, so rotate the bottle every so often to help them grow straight.

Your garden is a perfect, living, flourishing ecosystem. But what if you added a drop of poisonous liquid each day or continuously blew smoke into it through a straw? It wouldn't flourish very long. Why, then, do we allow chemical plants and pulp mills and litterbugs to pollute our environment? Good question.

Glass Game-Timer

How many times can you bounce a ball or skip a rope in sixty seconds? Make this glass game-timer and find out.

You'll need two matching, clear glass bottles that still have their tops. Short, squat containers, like the wide-mouthed Heinz Tomato Ketchup bottles, are best. In addition, you'll need a tube of strong glue, made especially for metals, and some clean sand or sugar or salt.

Unscrew the tops and wash out the bottles carefully, removing the labels at the same time. Set the bottles aside to drain until their insides are thoroughly dry.

While the caps are unscrewed, glue them together back to back. When the glue is dry, punch a small hole through the center of the tops with a nail. Now fill one of the bottles half full of the particles you are using and screw on the top. Screw on the other bottle and your game-timer is complete.

Test the time with a watch, adding or removing particles until it takes exactly one minute for them to pour from one bottle into the

other. A few grains will always remain behind in the cap, but this makes no difference. When you're satisfied, put some glue inside the rim of the tops to bond them permanently to the bottles.

Water Truck

This rugged truck carries a tank of water on its rear platform. Like the trucks that wash streets or water crops, it has a nozzle that can actually spray out water in all directions.

To make the truck, you'll need an 8½-inch length of 2 x 4, a 3-inch length of 2 x 4, four 1¼-inch-long spools, the spray nozzle from a Windex bottle, and some strong nails. In addition, you will need four large, matching coffee-jar tops, the plastic ones that come on Sanka, Maxim or Martinson Coffee. Finally, you will need a large glass bottle with a plastic top, such as a Chock Full O'Nuts instant-coffee jar.

Begin by gluing or nailing the short length of 2 x 4 onto the long one, as shown in the drawing, to form the cab and the back platform of the truck. Next, take the four matching plastic tops, which will be the wheels, and make a small hole in the center of each one. This is best done by gently boring into the plastic with a knife or pointed scissors. Put a long nail through the hole in each wheel, slide a spool onto each nail to act as a washer, and hammer the nails into the wooden

body of the truck. Leave enough space between the body and the spools so that the wheels can turn freely.

Remove the wire ends from a package handle and glue the wooden or paperboard roll to the front of the truck for a bumper. Add a belt buckle or pocket comb for a radiator grill and two bottle tops for headlights. The rear bumper and tail lights can be made from a package handle and red pushpins. The main part of the truck is now finished, and the only thing left to construct is the glass tank.

Bore a hole into the plastic top of the coffee bottle halfway between its center and one edge. Make the hole just big enough for the squirting mechanism from a Windex bottle to slide snugly through. Leave the paper lining inside the top to help prevent leaks. Using a waterproof glue that works well on both metals and plastics, stick the nozzle to the bottle top. Use lots of glue on the inside to make it watertight. After the glue is completely dry, fill the tank with water and screw the top on.

Drive two large nails partway into the back platform of the truck to make a slot for the tank, then load it on board. The tank can be held securely in place by a wide rubber band slipped over the bottle and under the bottom of the truck.

Push the plunger on the nozzle and water will shoot forth. Because your tank is made of glass, it is both waterproof and transparent, which means you won't need a gauge to tell you when it should be refilled—you'll be able to see for yourself.

Spin the Bottle

What would a chapter on glass be without Spin the Bottle! It's one of the oldest of the "courting games," and the most popular. It's played out in the open on school playgrounds at lunchtime and recess. It's played more quietly after school on a friend's back lawn. And it's played secretly in the evening at neighborhood parties. But don't think you'll really fool any adults. They know what's going on, because they, too, played this game, with their parents sneaking a look from the hallway. Though Spin the Bottle has been played for generations by young Americans, its origin is unknown. Like other folk customs and games, it is so old and so familiar as to seem to have no beginning. And if you try to trace it back to the earliest bottles, well, that won't help much either. Glass itself is very very old.

In the game a glass bottle becomes a matchmaker, pairing off couples in some strange kind of bottle logic that seems to work. Though no one knows just how many romances started with a spinning bottle, there is no doubt that the number is still rising.

The game begins with everyone sitting on the floor in a circle: boy, girl, boy, girl. A large, empty bottle is placed on the floor in the center of the circle and someone—anyone—gives it a quick spin. When the bottle stops, the person it points out becomes the first player. He or she must come into the center of the circle and spin the bottle once again.

This time, there are three things that can happen: (1) The bottle can choose a person of the opposite sex from the spinner, in which case the two must kiss each other, like it or not, in front of all the other players. After the kiss, the person selected by the bottle becomes the spinner. (2) The bottle can end up pointing between a boy and a girl, in which case those two must kiss and the spinner must spin again. (3) The bottle can point out a person of the same sex as the spinner, in which case the spinner is out of luck and loses his turn. He is replaced by the person the bottle selected, and left without so much as a peck on the cheek.

PLASTIC

Believe it or not, the story of plastic begins with a billiard ball! In 1863 the Pheland and Collander Company, manufacturers of billiard balls, offered a $10,000 prize to anyone who could develop an adequate substitute for natural ivory, the material from which billiard balls had always been made. Two young American brothers, John and Isaiah Hyatt, set out to win the prize. In 1870, by combining cellulose nitrate, camphor, and alcohol, they made Celluloid. It was the first synthetic plastic, and it was a winner.

The development of other plastics followed. They were made from both natural and synthetic resins; and through the application of heat or pressure or both, they could be formed into virtually any shape. The name "plastic," then, is appropriate: it is derived from plastikos, which in Greek means "fit for molding."

Today plastics are used for all kinds of containers. And the containers are amazingly convenient: they're lightweight, they can be molded with nozzles and handles and knobs that would be difficult to form in other materials, and they won't break when dropped on the bathroom floor.

Yet plastic containers are a problem because they are so difficult to get rid of. They are troublesome to compact; they are nearly impossible to recycle; and, worst of all, they are nondegradable, which means that they do not disintegrate or decompose after they are thrown away. They just sit alongside the highways for years on end, as good as new, permanent litter, until someone finally gets around to picking them up.

If you pick up a few, you'll find that plastic containers are great for making toys and games. They come in bright colors; they can be cut; they're waterproof. And once the toys are made, they'll last forever.

Bottle People

Plastic bottles are a lot like human beings. They come in all shapes and sizes, just as we do: short and fat or tall and skinny. That's why it's so easy to make them into bottle people.

Almost any bottle will do, as long as it has the shape and personality that is required. If you want to make the haughty Queen of Hearts from Alice's Adventures in Wonderland, for example, you can use an Ivory Liquid bottle or a Joy bottle; a container of All or Wisk suits the King of Hearts. Their soldiers can be fashioned from small containers of Comet or Ajax, with playing cards hung on the front and back for shields. Boraxo bottles are fine for Tweedle-Dum and Tweedle-Dee, or for that matter, any other good-natured fatties. You'll find dozens of other characters you can make in such stories as Winnie the Pooh, The Wind in the Willows, and Snow White.

To begin, think of the empty bottle as the main body of the character. Then make a hole on each side of the upper part of the body,

where the arms will join the shoulders. Make
the hole with a knife or with the point of a
pair of scissors, gently turning the blade in a rotary
motion. Don't apply too much pressure. The hole
should be about ½ inch in diameter.

Take a piece of thin cloth about the
size of a handkerchief and begin threading one
of its corners into one of the holes, as shown in
the drawing. With a pair of tweezers, reach in
from the other side and pull the cloth out through
the second hole. Continue pulling the cloth until
it is equal on both sides of the bottle. These
pieces will form the arms of the character. Now
reach into the neck opening and pull out the
center of the cloth to form the head.

Take each arm and turn back the
ends to make hands. Hold the hands in place with
pipe cleaners wound like bracelets around the
wrists. Adjust the cloth until the arms seem the
correct length in proportion to the rest of the body.

Make a sort of pocket out of the
cloth protruding from the neck and stuff it with
three or four paper tissues rolled into a ball. Wrap
the cloth smoothly around the tissues and tuck
the excess down into the back of the neck. A stitch
or two with a needle and thread will make the
head secure. Also stuff the arms with tissues to fill

them out. The eyes and mouth can be drawn
directly on the cloth, or a face can be drawn on
paper and then pasted on.

An alternative method for making
bottle people is to cut the arms out of paperboard.
Make a hole in each arm at its shoulder end. Slip
a length of pencil through the holes in the
bottle and slide an arm onto each end. Glue a
short piece of cork onto the pencil ends to hold
the arms in place. The head can then be made
from papier-mâché, as were the puppet heads
described on page 38.

Bottle Furniture

The wooden-crate house on page 17 will need lots of furniture. Thanks to plastic containers, you'll be able to produce it quickly and easily .

To make two big easy chairs and a lamp shade, for example, take a plastic bottle that has the general shape of the one in the drawing and mark it with a crayon as shown. Using a sharp knife, cut it carefully along the marked lines. The lower piece and the middle piece will become the chairs; the upper part, with the cap still in place, will become the lamp shade. Make the chairs comfortable by stuffing them with paper tissues or cloth. Make a base for the shade out of a wooden clothespin and a plastic bottle cap.

And try making a bed from a plastic bottle and a table from a big plastic cap. There are dozens of pieces you can build. Pretty soon you'll have to add an extra room onto your crate house just to put the furniture in.

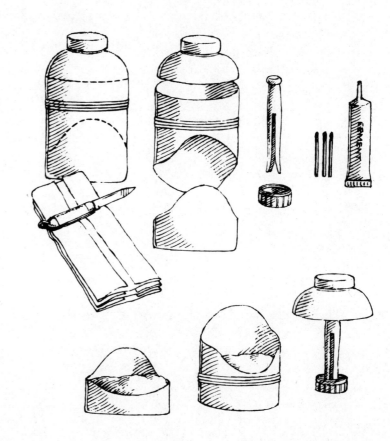

Plastic Pop Cannon

This latest advance in toy artillery can actually send paper missiles sailing fifteen feet through the air. It's perfect for defending the tin-can castle on page 110. With it you can easily repel clothespin soldiers advancing on your fortress; and you might even be able to ward off the airborne attacks of the terrible pterodactyl from page 34.

The pop cannon is made from a plastic bottle, which must be carefully selected. If the bottle isn't right, you'll have trouble constructing and firing your gun. The plastic must be soft enough to cut. The neck and mouth of the container must be about 1½ inches in diameter. Most plastic bottles have narrower mouths than this, but some can be cut off further down the neck to make a suitable opening.

One possibility is a plastic soda-pop bottle. Several soft-drink companies have begun to distribute their products in these bottles. Since some of them even look like old-fashioned cannon barrels, they are your best bet. The one used here was a Good-O Cola bottle.

Besides a suitable bottle, you'll need some plastic cup lids, the kind you get with take-out orders of hot coffee at a soda fountain. There are several different designs available. Try to get good strong white ones, molded to look like spoked wheels. You'll also need a pencil, two buttons, a rubber band, some long pipe cleaners, a knife, and a tube of glue that works well on plastics.

(1) To begin, first locate the molding line that runs lengthwise around the plastic bottle. It divides the container exactly in half, so it can be useful to you in your calculations. Follow this line about 1 inch down from the mouth of the bottle, and at this point make two small holes, one on each side of the bottleneck. A pointed knife or scissors ground into the plastic in an easy rotary motion works best.

(2) Take a rubber band and thread it through one of the holes. Slip a pipe cleaner through the outside loop to hold it in place, as shown in figure 1. Slip a second pipe cleaner through the other hole and use it as a hook to pull the rubber band out through that same hole (figure 1).

(3) Remove the hook and slip the first pipe cleaner around the barrel and through the loop of the band. The band is now held in place on both sides of the barrel by the pipe cleaner. Twist the

ends of the cleaner together so that it fits snugly around the barrel and break off any excess (figure 2).

(4) Make a small hole in the center of the bottom of the bottle. Link two long pipe cleaners together and thread them through the hole far enough so that one end projects through the mouth of the bottle. Slip the cleaner through one of the holes in a fairly large button, loop it over the rubber band, and then slip it back through another hole in the button (figure 3). Twist the cleaner around itself several times just behind the button (figure 3a).

(5) Pull the other end of the cleaner back through the bottom of the bottle and unlink the extra cleaner. It was there only to make sure you could get the first cleaner back through the hole. Hook a button onto the end of the first cleaner and twist the end around itself (figure 4). The length of the cleaner from button to button should be approximately equal to the length of the bottle. Your firing mechanism is now complete.

Wad up a paper ball about 1 inch in diameter and place it just inside the mouth of the barrel. Pull back the rear button, let go, and POW!

You can carry this hand-held pop

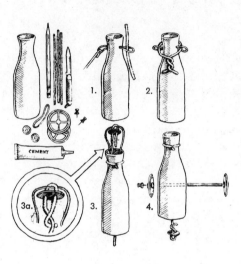

gun with you on dangerous missions. Or you can convert it into a rolling cannon simply by adding wheels.

Take the barrel in one hand, with your thumb and middle finger along the molding line on opposite sides of the piece. Move them back and forth until you find the point where the weight of the two ends is equal. This point is called the balance of the gun. Now move a little forward of that point so that the rear end swings down slightly, and mark the spot. Make a hole on both sides of the barrel big enough for a pencil to slide through easily.

Cut off the stem of a pencil about ½ inch longer than the width of the barrel. Slip this axle through the holes and glue each end to the center of a plastic-cup lid as shown in figure 4. Use lots of glue and hold each wheel in place with a plastic pushpin.

These wheels look fine, but they are not terribly sturdy. If you need stronger wheels, use coffee-bottle tops like the ones described on page 80. Slip a length of pencil through the cannon for an axle, glue a spool onto each end of the pencil, and then glue the spools to the inside of the coffee-top wheels.

You may find that the axle of the cannon inhibits the firing mechanism just a bit. If so, try pulling the interior button back only until it touches the axle, and no further. You may not get as much distance, but you will have fewer misfires.

Bottle-Cap Tiddlywinks

Bottles are usually sealed with plastic or metal caps which come in all sizes, colors, and shapes. They screw on; they twist off; they snap up. They are amazing little objects, but they are almost always tossed away without a glance as soon as the bottles are opened. Rescue a few from the trash and use them to play Bottle-Cap Tiddlywinks.

The field of play is constructed of two plastic-foam egg cartons, fitted into each other as shown in the drawing, and placed on a rug. The object is to use one bottle cap to snap another one up into the plastic egg pockets for the number of points that are marked on each pocket. The game is played on a rug in order to give the caps enough spring to jump into the carton.

Bottle-Cap Tiddlywinks is designed for play by two people sitting on opposite sides of the egg cartons, each with his own caps. The selection of caps is very important: some caps jump better than others, some caps snap better than others, and of course some caps are just luckier than others.

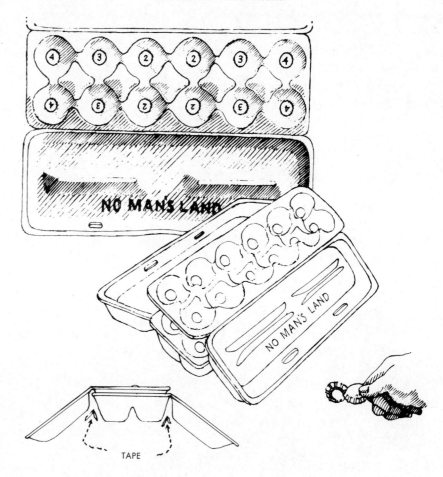

BOTTLE-CAP TIDDLYWINKS.

NO MAN'S LAND

NO MAN'S LAND

TAPE

To begin the game, one player snaps a cap into the carton. If his cap lands in a pocket, he gets the number of points marked on it, either two, three, or four; if it lands in "no man's land," he loses one point; if it lands off the board entirely, on the rug, he loses two points. It sometimes happens that a cap will end up between two pockets, balanced precariously on the edge. This is called a leaner, and it is worth a valuable five points. After finding out his score, the player removes his cap from the carton and the other player takes his turn.

Play continues with one snap per turn until one of the players has 21 points. He is the winner. But his score must be exactly 21. If he has 24, for example, he must manage to lose 3 points before he can win.

This is only one way to play. Try making up your own rules for a new game. And try designing a combination of egg cartons so that four people can play.

Bottle Banks

Now that you're making toys instead of buying them, you'll need a place to put the money you're saving. How about a piggy bank made from a Clorox bottle?

Take a medium-sized bottle and hold it on its side with the handle up and the cap pointing to the right. You'll discover a hog in hiding, with a fat white body and a sassy blue nose. Glue four large corks onto the underside for feet, stick a curly pipe cleaner through the backside for a tail, and glue two matching buttons onto the head for eyes. Cut two small pointed ears out of another plastic bottle and glue them to the head. Finally, cut a slit in the center of the back for coins to drop through.

At this point, you may begin to wonder about the horn formed by the handle on the pig's snout. What is an easygoing domestic pig like this one doing with such a big tusk? Your guess is as good as anyone else's. Maybe there's a romantic rhinoceros somewhere back in the family tree. In any case, the horn adds a touch of character that is sadly lacking in most other pigs.

A little piglet companion for the big pig can be made from two plastic-foam drinking cups. First tape the two open ends to each other with clear cellophane tape. Then glue four small cork feet on the underside and add a pipe-cleaner tail just the right length for a piglet. Glue on two button eyes, and with a felt-tip pen draw on eye lashes and a smiling mouth.

Many other animals can be found in the plastic bottles that line the grocer's shelves. For example, if you hold a Clorox bottle on its side with the handle down instead of up, it no longer resembles a pig with a horn but looks like a weasel with a buck tooth. And some of the bulkier bottles look like elephants with their snouts stuck in their mouths.

By varying the size and shape of the ears and the length of the legs, you can make a whole menagerie of different animals. Who would have guessed that the supermarket is really a zoo?

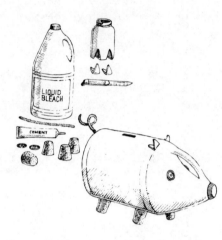

Plastic Space Station

Plastic clothespins, plastic glasses, plastic egg cartons, plastic caps and lids. Put them all together and you have a twenty-first-century outpost in space, an interplanetary research station complete with flying saucers, survival pods, and complex information-gathering equipment. You can build this space station indoors on the rug, or, even better, outside on the ground. There you can use stones to simulate the barren plains of Jupiter, or leafy plants to re-create the humid swamps of Venus. Ready for the countdown? Then dig deep into your supply of plastics and blast off.

There are about a million ways to build this space station; all of them will work, so detailed directions aren't necessary. Just follow the system outlined here, and then take off on your own, inventing new structures and new equipment to fill the needs of your particular space station.

You can begin by putting together a little astronaut from small corks, as in the drawing. If you don't have the corks at home, you can find packages of them at the dime store. If

you're lucky, you'll run across a gold button shaped like a ball to serve as a space helmet, like the helmets that NASA uses. To be in scale with the rest of the space station, your astronaut should be about 2¼ inches tall.

Since the exact nature of the terrain where the station will stand is unknown, most of the equipment should be built upon legs to hold it above any possibly hostile environments. Plastic clothespins, the kind with the metal springs, are perfect for these legs. Clip three of them onto an aerosol-can cap or a delicatessen container, add a little glue made especially for plastics, and you have a tripodal platform that can be the first unit of your station.

At this point you will need a number of plastic cup lids, the same kind you used to make the wheels for the pop cannon on page 91. Try to get white ones and try to get at least five or six of the same design, so that they will fit easily into each other. You can usually find plenty of them on the sidewalks outside drug stores.

Take one of your lids and glue it right side up on top of the three-legged platform you have just made. This effectively turns the platform into a landing pad for a flying saucer. To make the saucer, take a different kind of plastic lid, the translucent type that comes with cans of ground coffee, and glue a white cup lid on the top and a white cup lid on the bottom. Both of these cup lids should have their undersides facing up.

Now take a clear plastic glass, turn it upside down, and fit it into the upper cup lid of the saucer. Don't glue it on, since this clear cover will be removed and fitted over the astronaut each time he takes a trip in the flying saucer. You can make a seat for him inside by gluing a big plastic cap upside down in the middle of the white lid.

Not all the glasses and lids fit together, so you may have to experiment with several different combinations before you find one that works. Sweetheart Caps, number LP-508, and 10-ounce Raymer plastic glasses were used in the space station shown in the photograph.

Now settle the flying saucer onto the landing platform. Notice how the white lids on the saucer and on the platform interlock. In this manner energy can be fed from the platform into the saucer when it is at rest. If you glue a cup lid on the bottom of all the saucers in your fleet, they can always land at platforms like this one to be recharged.

The tallest point in your space station can be a nuclear generator tower made from three clothespins and three plastic glasses. Turn one of the glasses upside down and slip the clothespins onto it for legs. Take the second glass and glue its bottom to the bottom of the first one. Take the third glass and glue its top to the top of the second one. Stand the whole thing on its clothespin legs, place a colored plastic cap on the very top, and you have a clear, gleaming tower for your outpost in space.

To illuminate the station, put a lightning bug underneath the cap on top of the tower. And put one underneath a cap on each of your flying saucers. Fantastic. When it gets dark, your whole space station will vibrate with a strange yellow light.

Lightning bugs, by the way, are as unusual as any creature your astronaut is likely to encounter. The lantern of the firefly produces a light that is said to be "cold," because so little of the energy used in the process is converted into heat. This blinking light attracts bugs of the opposite sex. In fact, males and females of the same species have a characteristic flash that enables them to find each other.

Be sure not to glue down the plastic

SPACE STATION.

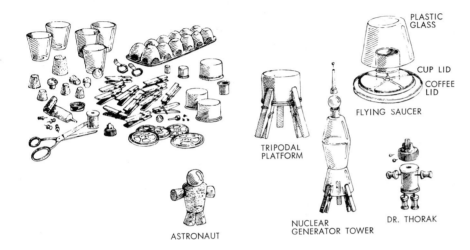

PLASTIC GLASS

CUP LID

COFFEE LID

FLYING SAUCER

TRIPODAL PLATFORM

ASTRONAUT

NUCLEAR GENERATOR TOWER

DR. THORAK

caps over the fireflies so you can let them go after a couple of hours. If you kept them, they would only die. Use them to illuminate your space station for a while, then help them on their way.

Lightning bugs are not the only unusual characters your astronaut will meet when he goes exploring. It's just possible that he will make the acquaintance of the interplanetary creature shown in the drawing. This bizarre fellow is made from a wooden spool, a plastic cap, and some pushpins; but in spite of these simple materials he has great powers, including a laser beam in his head. Luckily he is friendly. His name is Doctor Thorak, and he is one of the most respected citizens of this galaxy. The government of his planet has sent him to teach your astronaut about interplanetary conservation. Doctor Thorak and his people have seen what pollution has done to Earth, and they don't want the same thing to happen in outer space.

You now have Doctor Thorak for a guide, and lightning bugs to illuminate the way. Next, how about some survival pods? These pods provide storage space for food and equipment for the astronaut. They are made from egg cartons, preferably the white plastic-foam variety.

SPACE STATION.

SURVIVAL PODS

RADAR ANTENNA

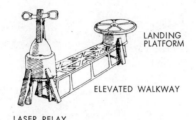

LASER RELAY

LANDING PLATFORM

ELEVATED WALKWAY

To make a cluster of pods, cut out the last four egg pockets from each end of a carton and trim them. Turn one group upside down and glue or tape it to the other, as shown in the diagram. Now cut out a single pocket and glue it on top of the cluster to form a pyramidal structure. Put a plastic cap on the very top to house the communication system.

You can use individual egg pockets to support other pieces of equipment. For example, clip a clothespin onto a plastic-cup lid, slip the other end of the clothespin through two slits in the top of an egg pocket, glue the pocket on one of your platforms, and you have a radar antenna. Slip two aluminum pop-top pulls into the clothespin in place of the cup lid and you have a laser-beam relay device. These pieces of equipment can be joined together by elevated walkways made from the plastic trays that tomatoes are packaged in.

The only thing your astronaut now lacks is a lunar rover, and you'll find a spool racer that can be used for one on page 22. And keep your eyes open for other things to add to your space station. The trash can is full of them.

METAL

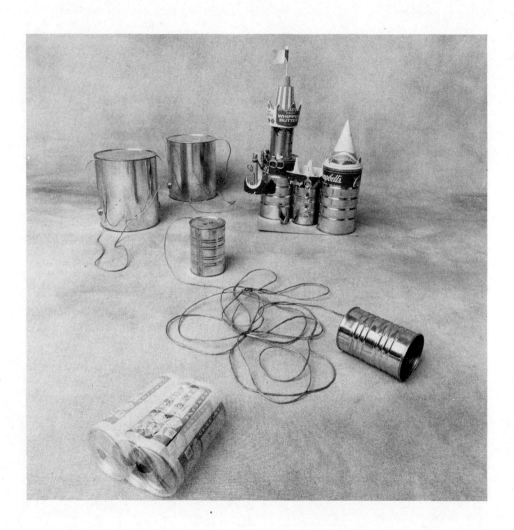

Metals have been so important in the development of society that whole periods of history, The Bronze Age, The Iron Age, are named after them. They have been used by man since 4000 B.C., when he first hammered lumps of copper into tools. We are still using them today, melting them in great blast furnaces and forming them into containers, machines, and building materials.

One of the most common metal objects is the can. It is so familiar that it seems as natural for holding food as the shell of an egg. It's hard to believe that the can is relatively new, that it was invented less than 200 years ago, at the beginning of the nineteenth century.

The early nineteenth century was a time of almost continuous warfare in Europe. People died not only in combat but also from malnutrition. Soldiers starved because there just wasn't any way to keep food fresh long enough to get it to them at the front. In hopes of finding a solution to this problem, the French government offered a prize of 12,000 francs to anyone who could discover a way to preserve food for long periods of time.

An obscure citizen, Nicolas Appert, worked on the problem for fourteen years. Finally, in 1810, he won the prize by showing that food sealed in an airtight container under extreme heat would not spoil. Though he used glass jars in his experiments, others soon developed metal containers similar to the ones we use today.

Neither Appert nor anyone else knew why this method was successful. It was not until fifty years later that Louis Pasteur, the French chemist, explained that microorganisms spoil food. Appert's method worked by killing them with heat. Recontamination was prevented by making the cans airtight.

Metal containers were originally called canisters. When they were introduced into the United States, however, Americans found the name too long, and they shortened it to "can." Since these steel containers were always covered with a thin layer of tin to prevent corrosion, they became known as tin cans.

Today there are several varieties of cans: those made of steel with a tin coating, those made of steel with a synthetic coating, and those made entirely of aluminum. Some new combination-cans have steel sides and aluminum tops. This mixing of materials has made recycling more difficult, since the different metals must be separated from each other before they can be reclaimed.

All varieties of cans work well for making toys and games. You can find them right in your own trash. When that supply is temporarily used up, just look outdoors, along the roadsides. You'll find plenty there. And you'll find metal wire and bottle caps and pop-top pulls as well. Take along a big corrugated box to put your metal finds in. You'll be loaded down in no time at all.

Tin-Can Stilts

104.

If you've ever wanted to be as tall as, say, King Kong, then metal cans may be the answer. All you'll need is two large cans of equal height and some sturdy cord. The cans will take quite a beating, so they should be strong. Steel cans are stronger than aluminum. And cans that have both ends in place are stronger than those that have one end removed. Large fruit-juice containers, which have been drained through puncture openings, are perfect.

      The first step in making toys out of cans is to slice off any half-opened lids or jagged edges with a good can opener. The lids should be put in the garbage to avoid cut fingers. Next remove any paper labels from the cans by making a vertical cut down the side of the paper and peeling it back in both directions. Often these labels are bright and colorful, so put them aside for use later on. Finally wash the cans out thoroughly with soap and water.

      To make the stilts, pierce a nail hole through opposite sides of each can very close to one end. Then take a cord and cut off two

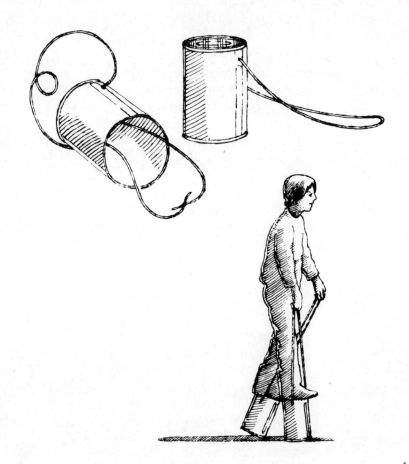

equal lengths, each long enough to reach from the level of your hips down to your feet and back again. Using a long pipe cleaner for a needle, thread a length of cord through the holes in one of the cans and tie its ends together to form a large loop. Do the same for the other can.

Now step up onto the stilts, one foot on each can. Suddenly you're a giant. Of course you'd be rooted in place if it weren't for the cords. Take one cord in each hand, pull tightly, and step out. If you don't let them drop, the cords will hold the cans snugly in place on your feet, and you can walk all over the neighborhood, pretending you're Kong or maybe Frankenstein. If you hear anyone mutter, "Here comes that tin-can freak again," just ignore him.

Tin-Can Walkie-Talkie

If you have confidential messages to send to a friend, messages too secret for the telephone, then a tin-can walkie-talkie is for you. All you need to make one are two medium-sized cans and a ball of good strong brown twine. The cans should each have one end opened and one end closed.

With a hammer and nail, make a single hole in the center of the closed end of each can. Now cut a length of twine equal to the distance you and your friend will be apart. If you're going to move from place to place while you're using the instrument, the line shouldn't be too long, since it has to be held out taut to work well. If the walkie-talkie is to be stationary, between two houses for instance, the line can be much longer.

Thread one end of the cord through the hole in the first can and the other end through the hole in the second. Tie a large knot in each end. Your tin-can walkie-talkie is ready for action. Stretch the line taut between you and your friend and speak into your can. If your friend

TIN-CAN WALKIE-TALKIE.

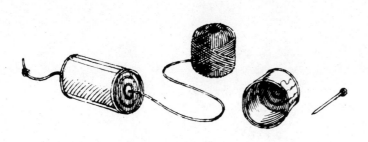

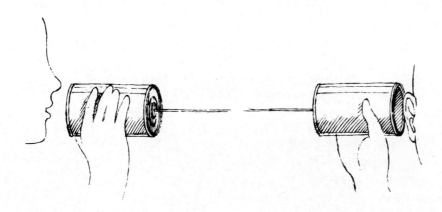

has his receiver to his ear, he'll understand every word you say. Try to keep the line from touching anything, since some of the sound is lost when it does. If you're not getting as much sound as you think you should, try waxing the twine.

If you're planning to use the walkie-talkie in a permanent location, you can make supports for the line by looping a cord around it and tying the loop to a tree limb or to whatever is convenient. The fewer supports you have, though, the less sound you will lose. If you like, you can run a second line along the same route with a small bell tied on each end of it; this can be used as a signal when you are making a call. Be sure the bell cord doesn't touch your main line.

Wonderful invention that it is, the tin-can walkie-talkie is not, however, foolproof. Like the standard telephone, it can be tapped. All some desperado needs is a tin-can receiver and a short cord. With the cord he can tie into your conversation at any point along the line. Have a secret code ready just in case.

Kick the Can

Kick the Can is the American name for a hide-and-seek game that uses a metal can as home base. The game is almost as widely known as are cans themselves. It's been played around the world since before World War I, in London as Tin Can Tommy, in New Zealand as Kick the Tin, in Italy as Barattolo, in France as La Boîte. It can be played with as few as four or five people, or with as many as the neighborhood can provide.

Place the can in the center of an open space and draw a circle around it on the ground. Choose a seeker by drawing straws or counting potatoes. Or, using the game-timer from page 79, time one minute during which all players search for pieces of litter. The person who comes back with the least will have to be the seeker. He will also have to gather up all the trash the others found and put it in a garbage can.

As soon as the seeker has been chosen, someone kicks the can out of the circle, and all the players scatter for the best hiding places they can find. The seeker must stay at the circle, with his eyes shut or blindfolded, until he counts to 100. He then retrieves the can, sets it up again in the circle, and begins to look for the hidden players.

As soon as the seeker discovers someone in hiding, he must shout a combination of words like "Tin can, tin can, one two three," followed by the name and location of the person he sees. At the same time he has to run like fury back to home base, put his foot on the can, and again call out, "Tin can, tin can, one two three." The player who was discovered is then considered a prisoner. He must stand beside the can until the end of the game or until he has been set free.

If the player is able to beat the seeker back to home base and kick the can, he can hide once more while the seeker is forced to count again to 100 and retrieve the can. By beating the seeker to the can, the player also sets free any prisoners, who can then hide again.

Prisoners can also be set free by any player who dares to sneak out of his hiding place and kick the can before the seeker can beat him to it. Thus, whenever the can is legally kicked by one of the hiders, all the prisoners are freed. In kicking the can, the hider should triumphantly yell, "Home free!"

The prisoners may also be freed whenever the seeker makes a mistake in naming the person whom he has discovered. If, for instance, he calls out, "Tin can, tin can, one two three! I see Jim Hoover behind the garage!" and it's really Cindy Stoverman who is lurking there, then a cry of "False alarm!" should spring up from the hiders, and all the prisoners should go free. For this reason, it's sometimes good strategy to exchange jackets or hats in order to trick the seeker.

After a while, of course, the poor seeker is at his wits' end, trying to roam far enough away to discover hiders while still attempting to stay near enough to home base to protect his prisoners. He is apt to become nervous and grouchy, and if you are a prisoner, you can shame him into taking chances by shouting insults, like:

"Leave the den, you dirty hen
And look for all your chickens!"

When everyone is captured, the game is over. But since that could take days and drive the seeker mad, you can end the game when all the prisoners have been released three times.

Mysterious Returning Can

In a survey of litter along a typical highway in the United States, 16 coffee cans, 90 oil cans, and 590 drink cans were found in just one mile!

When someone tosses a can onto a roadside, he thinks he's getting rid of the can. Of course he really isn't, because it always comes back to him in the form of visual pollution and higher clean-up taxes. If you know someone like this, you can show him the error of his ways with a mysterious can that rolls back to him whenever he tries to get rid of it.

To make this returning can, you'll need a heavy metal nut, a strong rubber band, and a pop-top can.

Begin by making a hole in the center of the bottom of the can with a nail. Thread a rubber band through the hole and slip a toothpick through the loop of the band to hold it in place, as shown in the drawing. Now fish down into the can for the other end of the band, using a pipe cleaner or a piece of wire for a hook. Pull the

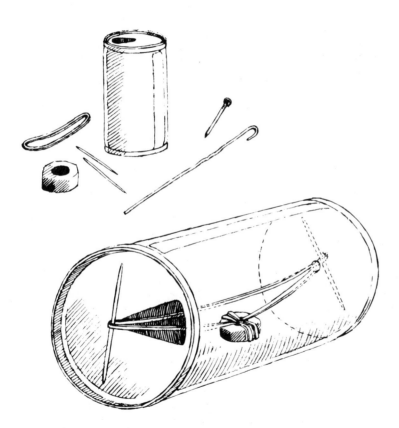

rubber band out through the pop-top opening and tie the metal nut onto one side of it. Slip a toothpick through the loop of the band to hold it and let the nut slip back into the can.

You now have a returning can. When you roll it away from you on a hard surface, the heavy weight inside does not go around, but winds up the rubber band instead. When the can comes to a halt, the elastic is wound up sufficiently to make it roll back to you . . . or to your favorite litterbug.

Tin-Can Castle

You'll need all the cans you can find for this one, plus clothespins, Quaker Oats boxes, toothpicks, bottle caps, corks, buttons, paper cups, egg cartons, and whatever else looks promising. Almost anything that people throw away can be used to build the towers and fortify the battlements of this shining, soaring, wonderful tin-can castle.

There are so many ways to build the castle that detailed instructions aren't really necessary. Anyway, you'll have your own ideas on how it should be done. One good way to start, though, is to take a large can with its label removed and put a smaller can on top of it. Then take a round cardboard container, like a Quaker Oats box, and cut the lower part off about 2 inches from the bottom. Cut it in a zigzag pattern so it will look like a medieval parapet. By using cardboard or plastic containers for the parts of the castle that need to be cut, you can avoid the more difficult job of cutting into metal.

Now place the part you have just cut on top of the smaller can, with the pointed ends up. Add a striped paper cup on the very top to

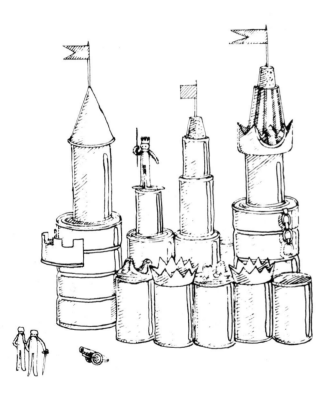

form a conical roof. Cut a semicircular balcony out of an ice-cream cup and glue it onto the side of one of the cans. You now have the first tower of your castle.

When you've built several towers, you will probably want to join them together to make an enclosure. You can do this with small soup cans lined up to form walls. On top of these rows place the bottom part of molded-pulp egg cartons. The ups and downs of these cartons provide good protection for soldiers between the towers.

When you have the various parts in a combination you like, make it permanent with a glue that will bond metal to metal. Then glue the whole castle down onto a large piece of stiff corrugated board to hold everything in place.

The towers are now ready to be festooned with flags and banners. These can be cut from can labels and pasted around toothpick flagpoles, as shown in the drawing. The poles can then be stuck into corks to hold them upright.

Tin-can towers look fine in their natural silver color, but you may want to paint the cardboard trim with poster paint. Red would be a good color. And you can cut out medieval-looking zigzag bands of color from your labels and paste them around the upper parts of the cans. It's your castle and you can make it just as colorful and festive as you like. Of course, if you want to build a second castle for the enemy, that fortress can be dark and somber with creepy battlements and evil dungeons and germs.

And now you have to consider the problem of defense. Castles do have to be defended because someone is always attacking them. King Arthur had to put up with it; Macbeth had to put up with it; and you will, too. Luckily, you can have all the defenders you need by making soldiers out of clothespins, as described on page 23. These soldiers are stouthearted; and if well trained, they will perform their duties with spit-and-polish precision.

To be completely effective, your army will need good equipment; and once again the trash basket can provide all you need: a toothpick with a bead at one end makes a sword; a button or a bottle cap serves as a shield; a cigar band quickly becomes a red and gold helmet.

In addition, a small cannon can be made from the cap end of a discarded, felt-tip pen. Just turn the clip side down, point the open end forward, and glue two bottle caps or two buttons on each side of the barrel to represent

wheels. Your soldiers can use the wire brush from an electric razor kit to clean out the cannon after each use.

It is possible that your men will be called upon not only to defend your castle but to storm some other fortress as well. Therefore, you will want to provide them with scaling ladders, which you can make by linking together the pulls from aluminum pop-top cans. You can smuggle spies into the enemy castle by hooking one of these chain ladders onto the rim of a tower when the guard is asleep. Of course, this could happen to you just as easily, so look with disfavor upon any guard found snoozing at his post.

A source of concern, too, will be the frequent airborne attacks of the terrible pterodactyl described on page 34. He takes fiendish pleasure in attacking tin-can castles, bombing them with bottle caps, nipping off their flags, even carrying away their heroic clothespin soldiers. He's in for a surprise, though, when you roll out your new secret weapon, the fabulous pop cannon from page 91. He just might find himself extinct again.

YOUR OWN IDEAS

YOUR OWN IDEAS

YOUR OWN IDEAS

YOUR OWN IDEAS